Rust Belt Chic:

The Cleveland Anthology

Second Edition

Edited by
Richey Piiparinen and Anne Trubek

First Printing, 2012
Second Edition, 2014

print version ISBN-13: 978-0-9859441-6-2
ebook version ISBN-13: 978-0-9859441-1-7

Belt Publishing
1667 E. 40th Street #1G1
Cleveland, Ohio 44120
http://www.beltmag.com

Book design by Haley Stone
Cover design by Haley Stone
Cover photo by Trudy Andrzejewski

In memory of Randall Tiedman

Table of Contents

III. History

IV. Growing Up

VII. Culture

VIII. Back Home

Acknowledgments

Contributors

About the Editors

Midst of a Burning Fiery Furnace

Let the foundries burn the whole city then.
Black the edges and the brazen joints.
Let the salamander sleep in his well of flame.
Because the worst has happened, and yet
so much more remains to be burnt,
smelt and milled and cast. These remains.
Suppose this blistered city would smolder
well after all those who live by the blast
of the furnace have left themselves to ash.
I have heard of that alchemy of steel—
I am familiar with the dying arts. Let them burn
the dark night livid, my poor republic
of ingot and slag. I am also seething
in my depths, I too have come to forge.

—Dave Lucas

Introduction to the Second Edition

Dave Lucas

> What can you say? The impossible happens.
> —Adam Again, "River on Fire"

Whatever *Rust Belt Chic is,* I'm for it.

I once bristled at the term "Rust Belt," corroded as it is with condescension toward this region, upon whose industries and industry other regions were built. I now find myself drawn to the phrase, as one's fingertips are drawn to a scar. In the midst of the present, we are marked by the past. We bear it everywhere we go. But mostly we bear it here at home.

Rust is remains. Rust makes tangible our ongoing and collective decay. But "chic" is a word for faddish novelty, something passing or already passed. "Rust Belt" goes with "chic" like iron goes with oxygen and water. As Joyce Brabner imagined it, "Rust Belt Chic" was the sound of the coasts sneering at a whole regional culture: "MTV people knocking on our door, asking to get pictures of Harvey [Pekar] emptying the garbage, asking if they can shoot footage of us going bowling." In the national media, Rust Belt Chic was supposed to be an oxymoron. In this anthology, it is a megaphone.

In these pages, "Rust Belt Chic" may by turns insult and honor; it might name a movement, an aesthetic, an attitude, a brand, or something else entirely. It might already be too shopworn to name anything specific at all.

Whatever else it has become, Rust Belt Chic is a way of speaking about Cleveland and other places like it. More importantly, Rust Belt Chic is a way for those of us who have lived in, who have loved and despised and obsessed over these places, to speak about ourselves. Rust Belt Chic means that our stories are worth telling, and that those stories will not be told for us.

Those pronouns—"our" and "us"—prove troublesome. As the editors of this anthology know, no single narrative—not even the tempting theme of rise and fall and resurrection—tells the story of the city. Stories clarify our experience and allow us to make meaning of it, but when they are reduced to sound bytes and slogans—"the mistake on the lake," "you've gotta be tough"—they lose their complexity.

It's too simple to say, with *Forbes* Magazine, that Cleveland is the most miserable city in the United States. Or to say, with *Fortune*, that Cleveland is the next Brooklyn, whatever that might mean. Too much of the writing about Cleveland is merely some version of such sloganeering elaborated to produce copy. Too much of it seems to have been written by tourist journalists on weekend assignment.

Provincialism thrives in the provinces, of course, but it's nurtured most lovingly in the capitals, where it masquerades as urbane charm. (Think of Saul Steinberg's brilliantly tongue-in-cheek *View of the World from 9th Avenue*). Thus, I suppose the Angeleno who told me, "I never knew there were so many hip people in Cleveland" intended it as a compliment. Thus, when *New York* magazine published its list of "what to do, where to stay, and what to eat in Cleveland" (after the announcement of LeBron James's return to the Cavaliers), a cultural critic for *Bloomberg Businessweek* cluelessly tweeted: "I assume this is just a link to a blank page."

But the urge to oversimplify persists here too. We see it in the commentary that appeals to Cleveland's supposed "authenticity" (as if other cities are somehow *inauthentic*) and in the penchant for reducing debates about the city to a false choice between "boosterism" and "critique." We see it in our collective elevation of professional athletes to the status of civic and cultural messiahs. And I see it in my own tendency to think of the region's sensibility as simultaneously fatalistic and defiant. It's easier, after all, to personify a city than to reconcile its contradictions.

I want to say that Clevelanders expect the worst, that they laugh at the worst when it happens, then collect the usable salvage from whatever wreckage remains in order to build again. I want to say that the urge to wander hums among us, as does the ache to return home. I want to say that within city limits, we're alternatively mordant and morbid about our home; take us away for too long and we wax sentimental.

But even this is too simple. No community of millions of people can be summed up in a few paragraphs, an essay, even an anthology. While I do find such fatalism and defiance in the pages of this anthology—often cut with a self-effacing gallows humor—I also find other impulses, other stories that do not fit my easy narrative. So I am grateful to the editors of this collection for their sensitivity to the work of telling as many stories as there are Clevelanders to tell them, and Clevelands to be told.

Whatever the current dominant narrative of the region may be—as told on the East or West coasts, or here on the North Coast, for that matter—the region's inhabitants ought to resist it. We've heard too much already about what we once were or what we're going to be from people who don't know who we are. We don't need more would-be sages at home who think they know the whole story. We simply need more stories.

Richey Piiparinen and Anne Trubek have produced something remarkable in *Rust Belt Chic: The Cleveland Anthology*. The essays collected here may well introduce even a lifelong Clevelander to otherwise unremarked aspects of the city's history and culture. These pages ward off easy conclusions—my own included—about what it might mean to be a Clevelander. The essays here speak for themselves, but they do not tell all that has happened since the publication of the first edition of this anthology in 2012.

The work that Anne and Richey began in this anthology, the work of allowing Clevelanders the voice and space to tell their own stories, continues both in the other two city-themed anthologies *Rust Belt Chic* has inspired (from Cincinnati and Detroit), and in the online magazine *Belt*, "devoted to long-form journalism, essay, and commentary with a distinctly Rust Belt sensibility." Taken together, *Rust Belt Chic* and *Belt* have led an emerging renaissance in the arts and letters of the region.

The continuing resonance of *Rust Belt Chic: The Cleveland Anthology* is evident in the remarkable fact that the book has sold through its first two printings. But its influence will be more lasting in less tangible ways. As new generations of Clevelanders look for opportunities to articulate themselves, they will have a book to read and reread, to treasure and argue with in their own words, in their own works.

The editors offer this second edition to continue and expand the conversation begun in 2012, especially by including several essays previously available only in the e-book edition. They have not asked the authors to edit or update these essays to reflect what has changed since the anthology was first published. Rather, this edition of *Rust Belt Chic* should serve as a document of its original moment as well as a way of speaking to the future of this region.

"This is no book," Walt Whitman wrote of *Leaves of Grass*. "Who touches this, touches a man." Who touches this, I hope, touches a city, becomes part of its many stories, begins to tell them anew.

The Cleveland Anthology

Introduction

R ust Belt Chic: The Cleveland Anthology provides an inside-out snap-shot of Cleveland. All the selections in this anthology take up, explicitly or implicitly, the idea of Rust Belt Chic, a concept that has been bandied about by developers, urbanists and journalists as a possible way to revitalize Cleveland and similar cities.

The book is descriptive, not prescriptive. It tells stories of who we are, not who we are promising or pretending to be. Cleveland is not perfect. But it has a distinct sense of place. And in a world of ever-growing ephemerality and superficiality, our authenticity is an asset. We need to be ourselves, if only to resist the temptation of trying to falsely re-brand ourselves.

America is in the grip of a budding "roots movement." Desires for the splashy are giving way to a longing for the past. Many are turning back toward the Rust Belt and geographies like it to find what they've been missing. Yes, the Rust Belt is a severe land, a disinvested land, a land of conflict. But it is also a land that lacks illusions and is full of real people, and that is becoming attractive to folks—be they returning ex-pats from Florida or young creative types tired of the bells and whistles of Global City, USA. This attraction is captured by the term "Rust Belt Chic."

Rust Belt Chic is churches and work plants hugging the same block. It is ethnic as hell. It is the Detroit sound of Motown. It is Cleve land punk. It is getting vintage t-shirts and vinyl for a buck that are being sold to Brooklynites for the price of a Manhattan meal. It is babushka and snakeskin boots. It is babushka in snakeskin boots. It is wear: old wood and steel and vacancy. It is contradiction, conflict, and standing resiliency. But most centrally, Rust Belt Chic is about home, or that perpetual inner fire longing to be comfortable in one's own skin and one's community. This longing is less about regressing to the past than it is finding a future through history.

The best revitalization efforts occur by bringing the past into the present—or by seeing what was there, understanding how it failed, and then integrating mistakes into a plan for the future. This is how individuals revitalize broken lives. It is a way for communities to revitalize broken cities, too.

And that's what this book is, too: a community effort to tell the story of a city. Inside these covers are narratives of failure, conflict, growth and renewal—the same themes we find in Cleveland. Our goal for this book is to retell Cleveland's story, to create a new narrative that not only incorporates but deepens and widens the familiar tropes of manufacturing, stadiums and comebacks.

Now, before we throw you into Cleveland, a little background on how the book came about. We put it together during the summer of 2012, prompted by hearing echoes of a Cleveland "resurgence" or "revitalization" on various national wires. We—two writers from different perspectives: one a born-and-bred West Sider, the other a recent arrival, living on the East Side—decided to tell the story from the inside-out rather than have it told by others, outside-in. The result is not pretty or shiny, but it is beautiful. It's a book about Cleveland after all.

—Richey Piiparinen and Anne Trubek *(2012)*

I. Concept

Randall Tiedman

Anorexic Vampires, Cleveland Veins: The Story of Rust Belt Chic

Richey Piiparinen

Rust Belt Chic is the opposite of Creative Class Chic. The latter [is] the globalization of hip and cool. Wondering how Pittsburgh can be more like Austin is an absurd enterprise and, ultimately, counterproductive. I want to visit the Cleveland of Harvey Pekar, not the Miami of LeBron James. I can find King James World just about anywhere. Give me more Rust Belt Chic.

—Jim Russell, blogger at *Burgh Diaspora*

In the spring of 2012, national interest in a Rust Belt "revival" blossomed. There were spreads in *Details*, *Atlantic Cities*, and *Salon*, as well as an NPR *Morning Edition* feature. And so many Rust Belters were beginning to strut a little, albeit cautiously—kind of like a guy with newly minted renown who's constantly poking around for the "kick me" sign, if only because he has a history of being kicked.

There's a term for this interest: "Rust Belt Chic." But the term isn't new, nor is the coastal attention on so-called "flyover" country. Which means "Rust Belt Chic" is a term with history—loaded even—as it arose out of irony, yet it has evolved in connotation if only because the heyday of Creative Class Chic is giving way to an authenticity movement that is flowing into the likes of the industrial heartland.

About that historical context. Here's Joyce Brabner, wife of Cleveland writer Harvey Pekar, being interviewed in 1992, and introducing the world to the term:

> I'll tell you the relationship between New York and Cleveland. We are the people that all those anorexic vampires with their little black miniskirts and their black leather jackets come to with their video cameras to document Rust Belt chic. MTV people knocking on our door, asking to get pictures of Harvey emptying the garbage, asking if they can shoot footage of us going bowling. But we don't go bowling, we go to the library, but they don't want to shoot that. So, that's it. We're just basically these little pulsating jugular veins waiting for you guys to leech off some of our nice, homey, backwards Cleveland stuff.

Now to understand Brabner's resentment we step back again to 1988. Pekar—who is perhaps Cleveland's essence condensed into a breathing human—had been going on Letterman. Apparently the execs found Pekar interesting, and so they'd periodically book Pekar—a file clerk at the VA—giving him the opportunity to promote his comic book, *American Splendor*. Well, after long, the relationship soured. Pekar felt exploited by NYC's life of the party; his trust in being an invited guest gave way to the realization he was just the jester. So, in what would be his last appearance, he called Letterman a "shill for GE" on live TV. Letterman fumed. Cracked jokes about Harvey's "Mickey Mouse magazine" to a roaring crowd before apologizing to Cleveland for . . . well . . . being us.

Think of this incident between two individuals—or more exactly, between two realities: the famed and fameless, the make-up'd and cosmetically starved, the prosperous and struggled—as a microcosm for regional relations, with the Rust Belt left to linger in a lack of illusions for decades.

But when you have a constant pound of reality bearing down on a people, the culture tends to mold around what's real. Said Coco Chanel: "Hard times arouse an instinctive desire for authenticity."

And if you can say one thing about the Rust Belt—it's that it's authentic. Not just about resiliency in the face of hardship, but in style and drink, and the way words are said and handshakes made. In the way our cities look, and the feeling the looks of our cities give off. It's akin to an absence of fear in knowing you aren't getting ahead of yourself. Consider the Rust Belt the ground in the idea of the American Dream.

Of course this is all pretty uncool. I mean, pierogi and spaetzle sustain you but don't exactly get you off. Meanwhile, over the past two decades American cities began their creative class crusade to be the next cool spot, complete with standard cool spot amenities: clubs, galleries, bike paths, etc. Specifically, Richard Florida, an expert on urbanism, built an empire advising cities that if they want creative types they must in fact get ahead of themselves, because the young are mobile and modish and are always looking for the next crest of cool.

These "Young and the Restless"—so they're dubbed—are thus seeking and hunting, but also apparently anxious. And this bit of pop psychology was illustrated in the piece "The Fall of the Creative Class" by Frank Bures:

> I know now that this was Florida's true genius: He took our anxiety about place and turned it into a product. He found a way to capitalize on our nagging sense that there is always somewhere out there more creative, more fun, more diverse, more gay, and just plain better than the one where we happen to be.

After long—and with billions invested not in infrastructure, but in the ephemerality of our urbanity—chunks of America had the solidity of air. Places without roots. People without place. We became a country getting ahead of itself until we popped like a blowfish into pieces. Suddenly, we were all Rust Belters, and living on grounded reality.

Then somewhere along the way Rust Belt Chic turned from irony into actuality, and the Rust Belt from a pejorative into a badge of honor. Next thing you know, banjo bingo and DJ Polka are happening, and suburban young are haunting the neighborhoods their parents grew up in before leaving. Next thing you know, there are insights about cultural peculiarities, particularly those things once shunned as evidence of the Rust Belt's uncouthness, but that were—after all—the things that rooted a history into a people into a place.

Take the Pittsburgh Potty. For recent generations it was about the shame of having a toilet with no walls becoming the pride of having a toilet with no walls. From *Pittsburgh Magazine*:

> We purchased a house with a stray potty, and we've given that potty a warm home. But we simply pretended as if the stray pot-

ty didn't exist, and we certainly didn't make eye contact with the potty when we walked past it to do laundry.

The Pittsburgh Potty is basically a toilet in the middle of many Pittsburgh (and Cleveland) basements. No walls and no stalls. It existed so steel workers could get clean and use the bathroom without dragging soot through ma's linoleum.

Authentic: Yes. Cool? A toilet?

Only in the partly backward Rust Belt of Harvey Pekar and friends. From the feed of @douglasderda who asked "What is a Pittsburgh Potty?" Some responses follow:

"I told my wife I wanted to put ours back in, but she refused. I threatened to use the stationary tubs."

"In my house, that would be known as my husband's bathroom."

"It's a huge selling feature for PGH natives. I'm not kidding. We weren't so lucky in our ... home."

"We're high class people. Our Pittsburgh Potty has a bidet. Well, it's a hose mounted on the bottom, but still . . . ."

Eventually, this satisfaction found in re-rooting back into our own Rust Belt history has become the fuel of wisdom for even Coastal elites. Here's David Brooks talking about the lessons of Bruce Springsteen's global intrigue being nested in the locality that defines Rust Belt Chic:

If your identity is formed by hard boundaries, if you come from a specific place ... you are going to have more depth and definition than you are if you grew up in the far-flung networks of pluralism and eclecticism, surfing from one spot to the next, sampling one style then the next, your identity formed by soft boundaries, or none at all.

Brooks continues:

The whole experience makes me want to pull aside politicians and business leaders and maybe everyone else and offer some pious advice: Don't try to be everyman . . . . Go deeper into your own tradition. Call more upon the geography of your own past. Be distinct and credible. People will come.

And some are coming back to Cleveland, albeit slowly, unevenly. But more importantly, as a region we are once again becoming—but nothing other than ourselves.

Authenticity, reality: This was and always will be the base from which we wrestle our dreams back down to solid ground.

American splendor, indeed.

The Revenge of the Pittsburgh Potty

Jim Russell

I *am from Erie*. And I know this is a book about Cleveland. But to understand how the Rust Belt Chic of Cleveland came about you need to know the historical inelegance of Pittsburgh. But don't worry. You are most likely from the Rust Belt. So you already do.

The Rust Belt is a place you leave. Loserville (your hometown) is ubiquitous in America's industrial heart. In fact, thanks to the infamous exodus of the 1980s, Pittsburgh was the definition of "brain drain." That mythological landscape served as the muse for the urban strategist Richard Florida's Creative Class enterprise. Life was elsewhere, namely in Austin. Slackers were cooler than Yunzers.

In May 2002, Florida published an article in the Washington Monthly titled, "The Rise of the Creative Class: Why cities without gays and rock bands are losing the economic development race." Pittsburgh (and by association, Cleveland) is the example of what not to do:

> Even as places like Austin and Seattle are thriving, much of the country is failing to adapt to the demands of the creative age. It is not that struggling cities like Pittsburgh do not want to grow or encourage high-tech industries. In most cases, their leaders are doing everything they think they can to spur innovation and high-tech growth. But most of the time, they are either unwilling or unable to do the things required to create an environment

or habitat attractive to the creative class. They pay lip service to the need to "attract talent," but continue to pour resources into recruiting call centers, underwriting big-box retailers, subsidizing downtown malls, and squandering precious taxpayer dollars on extravagant stadium complexes. Or they try to create facsimiles of neighborhoods or retail districts, replacing the old and authentic with the new and generic—and in doing so drive the creative class away.

Pittsburgh is guilty as charged. There were stadium boondoggles and a casino, as well as a theater district. The city was desperate to keep Carnegie Mellon University graduates from fleeing to Austin. Yet the region remained unattractive to the Creative Class. The rock band Styx performing "Renegade" at Steelers games wasn't gay enough.

In 2004, Richard Florida did what most Pittsburghers with college degrees still do—move to Washington, DC. His stint at George Mason University was short-lived. He landed a dream job at the University of Toronto in 2007. Here was another superstar who had to get out of Pittsburgh in order to make it big.

Creating Cool

"Don't be a Pittsburgh." The slogan resonated across the country. In 2003, then-Michigan Governor Jennifer M. Granholm took up the gauntlet thrown down by Richard Florida. Her state's cities would be Creative Class chic. From the "Michigan Cool Cities Report":

The Cool City banner is a fun way to describe a very serious mission. To thrive in the future, Michigan cities must attract urban pioneers and young knowledge-workers who are a driving force for economic development and growth. These individuals are mobile and we want them to consider, and then choose, Michigan cities. To do this, we need to change some of our old ways of thinking by making quality of place a major component of economic development efforts.

Cities and regions with large numbers of urban pioneers, or what author Dr. Richard Florida describes as the "Creative Class," are thriving. Build a cool city and they—young knowledge workers and other creative class members—will come.

Build what, exactly? To this day, the program remains a mystery. Attracting the Creative Class is a black box. Back to Florida's drawing board sketched in the *Washington Monthly*:

> Over the years, I have seen the community try just about everything possible to remake itself so as to attract and retain talented young people, and I was personally involved in many of these efforts. Pittsburgh has launched a multitude of programs to diversify the region's economy away from heavy industry into high technology. It has rebuilt its downtown virtually from scratch, invested in a new airport, and developed a massive new sports complex for the Pirates and the Steelers. But nothing, it seemed, could stem the tide of people and new companies leaving the region.
>
> I asked the young man with the spiked hair why he was going to a smaller city in the middle of Texas—a place with a small airport and no professional sports teams, without a major symphony, ballet, opera, or art museum comparable to Pittsburgh's. The company is excellent, he told me. There are also terrific people and the work is challenging. But the clincher, he said, is that, "It's in Austin!" There are lots of young people, he went on to explain, and a tremendous amount to do: a thriving music scene, ethnic and cultural diversity, fabulous outdoor recreation, and great nightlife. Though he had several good job offers from Pittsburgh high-tech firms and knew the city well, he said he felt the city lacked the lifestyle options, cultural diversity, and tolerant attitude that would make it attractive to him. As he summed it up: "How would I fit in here?"

Pittsburgh tried everything to be cool. It didn't work. The prescription for urban success was always vague. The emperor had no clothes. Either your city was Creative Class chic or it wasn't. Pittsburgh was stuck in the latter category.

Cool All Along?

In May 2002, an economist at the University of Pittsburgh took issue with Richard Florida's brain-drain narrative. Chris Briem published an opinion piece in the *Pittsburgh Post-Gazette* titled, "Young people are NOT leaving Pittsburgh: Statistics in hand, Chris Briem is happy to explode the myth of a continuing exodus." Apparently, the Creative Class has an unusual tendency to stay in Pittsburgh:

> The rate of younger workers fleeing the region is a small part of the change in population. The rate of net migration of those in their 20s is perhaps something on the order of 0.1 percent per year, a very small fraction of what it was 15 years ago. That means for every thousand 20-somethings we count here this year, we will expect to count 999 a year from now. Is that what we are getting so upset about?

A typical out-migrant was over 65, probably lacking a college degree (if not a high school diploma). Not exactly your dance club regular. Pittsburgh's population was shrinking, but not for the reasons Richard Florida was touting.

Fortunately for Florida, no one believed Briem. Communities lined up to learn how to get out of the Pittsburgh trap. You too can put the lid back on hell. Little did anyone know, hell with the lid taken off was cool.

From a travelogue in *Atlantic Monthly*, 1868:

> There is one evening scene in Pittsburg which no visitor should miss. Owing to the abruptness of the hill behind the town, there is a street along the edge of the bluff, from which you can look directly down upon the part of the city which lies low, near the level of the rivers. On the evening of this dark day, we were conducted to the edge of the abyss, and looked over the iron railing upon the most striking spectacle we ever beheld . . . It is an unprofitable business, view-hunting; but if anyone would enjoy a spectacle as striking as Niagara, he may do so by simply walking up a long hill to Cliff Street in Pittsburg, and looking

over into—hell with the lid taken off.

The blog *AntiRust* noted the negative connotations that had been tied to the phrase "hell with the lid taken off" for some time. Little do people know, it was meant as a comment of praise, not condescension.

> The writer is describing the view, molten wreaths of fire, as far as the eye can see; not the livability of the city, the cuisine, the people, or anything else. "Here," he wrote, "all is curious and wonderful; site, environs, history, geology, business, aspect, atmosphere, customs, everything . . . . To know Pittsburg thoroughly is a liberal education in the kind of culture demanded by modern times." It was practically a love letter to the city, yet that damned "hell with the lid taken off" line is all that survives.

This was the birth of Rust Belt Chic.

Steel Valley Chic

Randy Fox is my favorite Rust Belt Chic photographer. I'm drawn to the same images he captures. I admire the same artists he shares with his audience at his blog, *American Elegy*. What is so captivating about those pictures? Rust Belt Chic is like ruin porn. I know it when I see it.

Akin to James Parton's strange love letter to "Pittsburg," Fox celebrates "steel valley chic" cinema (e.g. *Deer Hunter*) from the local's perspective:

> *Reckless* was set in Weirton, W. Va., and was largely filmed there, as well as in Steubenville, Ohio (right across the bridge from Weirton) and Mingo Junction. While still formulaic and marketed as a teen flick, *Reckless* was a cut above the Tom Cruise steeltown tale, *All The Right Moves*, which was filmed in Johnstown, Pa.
>
> In his inaugural starring role, Aidan Quinn somehow made sense in his role as Johnny Rourke, Reckless' angry factory-town rebel with an alcoholic mill-working father. Johnny Rourke worked for us because we understood why he hated his surroundings—and maybe we also knew that he wouldn't be the

sort of cool, fucked-up and even romantic catastrophe that he was without those very surroundings.

Those very surroundings give birth to fucked-up cool. "Chic" is as ironic as comparing the "Pittsburg" inferno to the awesome splendor of Niagara Falls. The romantic catastrophe is a hero. That slag heap dump of a town is beautiful.

Voila, Rust Belt Chic.

Rust Belt Chic New York City

The US urban revival over the last 40 years started in New York. During the 1970s, the Big Apple was as bad as Mingo Junction. Artists of that time and place, such as Robert Smithson and Ray Mortenson, developed the aesthetic of urban decay. This was ruin porn NYC, the South Bronx. You now know how cosmopolitan hipsters developed a taste for authentic Cleveland.

Seeing a bit of the South Bronx in Cleveland is not a compliment. Some might call it ruin porn. Joyce Brabner, the wife of Cleveland's late poet laureate Harvey Pekar, bitingly termed it "Rust Belt Chic."

The first mention of "Rust Belt Chic" I can find—Joyce Brabner's, cited in the previous essay—is a pejorative. New York is at the wrong end of the barb. It shouldn't be. The center of all that is Creative Class Chic had to be Rust Belt Chic first. Cleveland didn't appreciate playing second fiddle. Perhaps because in the birth of cool it's really Rust Belt DNA imprinted on New York.

So, you want the real deal? Come to the factory coast. Here's Anthony Bourdain, a NYC staple and booster of bat-shit-crazy New York, eulogizing Pekar:

> After all, Cleveland, the city he lived in and loved, had, he reminded us, lost half its population since the 1950s. A place whose great buildings and bridges and factories had once exemplified 20th century optimism needed its Harvey Pekar.
>
> "What went wrong here?" is an unpopular question with the type of city fathers and civic boosters for whom convention centers and pedestrian malls are the answers to all society's ills. But Harvey captured and chronicled every day what was—

and will always be—beautiful about Cleveland: the still majestic gorgeousness of what once was—the uniquely quirky charm of what remains, the delightfully offbeat attitude of those who struggle to go on in a city they love and would never dream of leaving.

What a two-minute overview might depict as a dying, post-industrial town, Harvey celebrated as a living, breathing, richly textured society.

That "majestic gorgeousness of what once was" is Rust Belt Chic. That, not tolerance, informs the uniquely quirky charm that can and has attracted the Creative Class. From a Pittsburgh Potty will spring the throngs of the sexually ambivalent at nightclubs. And someone like Anthony Bourdain will lament the passing of a time when a city was cool, way back in 2002 when Shittsburgh last owned a piece of American splendor.

Richard Florida's Pittsburgh didn't need to be more tolerant, more like Austin. Austin needed to get weird, more like Pittsburgh. The Rust Belt mistake was chasing Creative Class Chic to solve a brain-drain problem that didn't exist. The answers to chronic recession and demographic decline were always right in front of you. New York City circa 1970 is Cleveland today. Rust Belt Chic.

II. Snapshot

Bob Perkowski

Pretty Things to Hang on the Wall

Eric Anderson

I *want to laugh* when I hear that people are moving to Cleveland to practice their art. Then I want to spit in their faces. I want to do them grievous bodily harm. How dare they, I think. The nerve. Cleveland has never been the kind of place where it's easy to be an artist; in fact, people who want to unravel the greater mysteries or search for universal beauty or answer the unanswerable questions usually leave Ohio, while those who stay often find themselves using art as a way to make life on the North Shore more bearable. In Cleveland, there just aren't that many careers in the arts to be had. When I told my father I was thinking about going to the Cleveland Institute of Art, he said, "What kind of work can you find doing that?"

In fairness, he knew I lacked any sense of practicality. I wasn't thinking about a career in graphic design. I wanted something like Warhol, but you know . . . more manly. But I was young and I didn't have an answer to his question, so I did what he did. I found a job working construction in the steel mills.

When my artist friends talk about the dangerous toxicity of things like cadmium red and sprayable fixative, I nod politely but inside I'm cracking up. During my time as a surveyor in the mills, traveling back and forth between what was then US Steel in Lorain and LTV in

Cleveland, I used to see water so polluted that nothing would float in it. I would see dead rats with tumors exploding out of their sides. The old timers would tell me how much dirtier the mill used to be, before the hippies, before the EPA. The cars in the parking lot would be covered in red dust. Open your lunch box, red dust on the food. Spit, red dust. Cough, red dust. After a rain, the gutters were streaked with something that looked like dried blood.

When I was a boy, my father would come home from the mill and wash his face and hands in the sink; I would tell him about my small day and watch the water turn brown as it swirled. When he was done he would wipe his face on the towel and leave behind the imprint of a red skull; he couldn't wash enough to get clean.

I had a romantic notion that such filthiness was what it meant to be a man. But after a few weeks in the mill, I started dreaming about cancer. There was a story about some geese that landed in the vivid green wastewater-retention basin and sank right to the bottom. I'd imagine my body after death, completely decayed, only a man-shaped pile of rust in my coffin.

Those dreams weren't enough to stop me from going to work though. From my late teens—in those days when we weren't all pretending a college education matters—until my mid-thirties when I decided that a master's degree in fiction and poetry would somehow make my life better, I kept willingly walking into mills and factories and industrial complexes. Usually these excursions would begin with a brief safety video describing all the ways one was likely to be killed inside. The names on the mills changed: US Steel became USS/Kobe, and LTV, which the old timers used to call "Good old Liquidate, Terminate, and Vacate," closed and opened and morphed around before becoming ArcelorMittal. Each time the names changed, fewer people had jobs.

The name that has stayed with me the most came from LTV: the Continuous Annealing Line. Annealing is a process by which steel is heated and then slowly cooled so that the metal will be tough. Imagine being annealed continuously.

In those spare moments when I wasn't sweating a mortgage

payment or trying to coax some education for my children out of the region's essentially rotten school system, I pretended to be an artist. In school, I was only interested in art and English, and after graduation I clung to those two things as a justification for why I was wasting my life working construction all over Northeast Ohio. I fancied myself as one of those artists who would speak for common people, never really imagining myself as one of the commoners. The most consistent thing in my life was the terrible impracticality of my art. I wrote novels and sent poems to the *New Yorker*. On job sites, I would collect materials and wire them into sculptures—it's hard to be discreet when you're wiring rebar and scraps from the carpenter's forms into things that look a little bit like birds. Draw a little on the back of a pay stub, paint with a set of cheap watercolors from Pat Catan's. If anyone asked, I would curse my art by calling it a hobby. To be a native-born artist in Cleveland, you must master the art of self-deprecation. You must not let the normal folks know that you have been thinking, now and then, about immortality.

Of course, the newcomers mean well. They have come from other places in the country where it's too hard to be an artist; perhaps the grant money ran out, or the colleges are only hiring adjuncts. It could be that the inspiration just disappeared, as inspiration sometimes does.

Since it's so hard to be paid to live as an artist in Cleveland, the aspirant lives somewhere cheap. This neighborhood usually features a housing project and some boarded-up factories. Someone calls an abandoned warehouse a loft. A few more artists show up, and someone opens a gallery. Soon there's a coffee shop and a diner and a Laundromat. Other people who have artistic temperaments arrive; a few of them mean well, but most of them call themselves artists despite the lack of any real talent. They want to be artists the same way that sports fans want to play shortstop for the Yankees. Instead of skill, they have disposable income. They have investments and trust funds. The coffee shop becomes a Starbucks, the diner an Applebee's. The prices in the galleries reflect what everyone's calling "the growing importance of the movement."

The first sign of the coming apocalypse is the art walk: the Typhoid Marys of gentrification. Developers show up, displaying all the sensitive charm of a multinational corporation. The first thing they fix is the parking situation. They refurbish the factories because that's the kind of news that looks good in the arts section, and they evict the last surviving members of the original neighborhood, the old immigrants and housing project leftovers because that's the kind of story that appears in a blurb at the back of the city section. Rent goes up. The air is thick with the smell of money. Money smells like being neighbors with a bread factory. Sure, you want to believe that's what heaven smells like. But really, breathing has become a long struggle against yeasty suffocation. Meanwhile, the artists can no longer afford to stay in the neighborhood, and nobody knows what happened to the people who lived there before—shadows remain, or a few splotches of paint in the background of somebody's landscape.

But it's all OK. There's a lot of good space further out on the West Side or the East Side, cheap rent, a Salvation Army. Everyone's moving there.

It was never really about art. The artists wanted whatever it is that artists want (recognition, a solo show, a mention in a textbook, a cash award, a residency, a sabbatical, to be called a genius by people that other people call geniuses, anything but a job), and the gallery owners made a little money—which they used to pay back their loans, which means the banks made some money, and some developers got rich. People looking for ways to be young and hip and successful mortgaged ridiculously expensive townhouses and brownstones and bought pretty things to hang on the wall. Hanging things on the wall meant decorating the room. Contractors were hired, supplies were ordered, and workmen were paid. How it all trickles down so beautifully! I try my best to believe that, even if only by accident, some human looked at something made by another human and wondered what it all meant.

It's all understandable, and it's shitty, but I can get over that. What I can't and won't get over is how the artists swaggered into town like Major Leaguers going down to the minors on a rehab assignment. While I spent my time being afraid to want something beautiful, they actually went to art school. Some of them arrived here with a certain kind of fame. Some of them didn't become famous until they saw what we've done to ourselves. Along the way, they dragged a few natives into the brief, burning spotlight. I try not to be jealous. But it's too easy to hate the truly talented. Or the truly connected. Or the lucky.

It's hard not to feel like the details of my working life became their art. All that beautiful decay they seemed to say. Look at how wonderful this place used to be. Look at how terrible it all was. This region really says something about the world. This says something about our nation. I feel like I've lived here all my life!

I feel guilty for overstating the problem. Then I feel like I am not overstating the problem at all. They came and looked at my secret fears and told me how interesting they are, and how relevant, and how all that misery makes such a fascinating mosaic, if only I could step back and see how all the details have been arranged.

Yet none of them asked where the rust came from.

There's no way of knowing in the end what matters more: the lives that those mills and factories supported or the art that only exists because those lives no longer exist. In the end, it's not the fact that I or my friends and family feel exploited. It's not that the visiting artists were wrong or even that they were right. What most bothers me is that I wasn't smart enough to exploit the situation for myself. The whole thing was happening all around me, and I was too busy watching what I imagined as real artists watch and document what I called home. All those moments of folly when I gave up my ambitions to pay the bills. All those things that flashed briefly beautiful before I pushed them aside. It all turned out to be art after all. I just missed it.

Pilgrim's Progress

Pete Beatty

> I confess this side of the country was much pleasanter than mine; but yet I had not the least inclination to remove, for as I was fixed in my habitation it became natural to me, and I seemed all the while I was here to be as it were upon a journey, and from home.
>
> —Daniel Defoe, *Robinson Crusoe* (1719)

I *'m from Berea*, a small college town in southwestern Cuyahoga County and a particle in the million-mile suburban tundra of greater North America. I like to think of Berea as a small college town that got gobbled up by sprawl, as opposed to just another suburb. Berea is small and it has a college in it, so I'm not actively lying. I am sure everyone from Westlake or Bay or Maple Heights or Euclid has a little homiletic brain loop they recite when trying to differentiate their hometown from the aluminum-siding kudzu that makes up most of greater Cleveland. I am sure everyone from everywhere clutches some small poetry about why their hometown is misunderstood and secretly delightful.

It would be actively fudging a little to say that Berea is an inner-ring suburb, or to round down my roots and say that I'm from Cleveland proper. My family is respectively from the exurbs of Toledo and the edges of Cuyahoga County, pretty much as far back as it matters. Before that they were farming dirt somewhere in early modern Europe. In general, I am proud that my people were suburbanites before white flight debased that status. We were out in the suburbs for air show disasters and the old Browns training camp, before notions like Crocker Park and the dollar-menu McMansions of Strongsville made the fringes of the county even less sexy than they are now. I'm more or less proud to be from Berea. But I wasn't born there.

I opened my eyes for the first time at Southwest General Hospital in Middleburg Heights, elevation 850 feet, a sub-urbanity that is a non-place, just like all the other non-places that surround every decent-sized city. When I was a kid, the stretch of Bagley where I was born was just the hospital and a small amount of nothing littered with some isolated houses, a car dealership, the K-Mart, a few fast-food spots, and the Holiday Inn where my aunt worked. Now all sorts of nothing line both sides of the road: gas stations, many more chain restaurants, a shuttered car dealership, a strip mall. The Taco Bell was torn down and replaced with a new Taco Bell, built to keep pace in the arms race with Chipotle. Around the corner from K-Mart, there's something called Penn Station East Coast Subs, that as of a couple years ago still had an autographed picture of Tim Couch on the wall (Note: I have been to Penn Stations in New York City, Baltimore, and Newark, and none of them are the kind of place that you should name a restaurant after).

Back to my sketches of provincial life: What was a craft supply store next to the K-Mart now sells guns, which seems like a troubling index of cultural drift. A few thousand feet west of the hospital, there's a funeral home that used to be a Golden Corral, which itself used to be a benignly pointless spread of land next door to Pizza Hut (which has always been Pizza Hut). Just across the road, there's a shopping center with a Panera and an Aldi and a Regal Cinemas multiplex. Despite that novelistic detail of a funeral home that used to be a bulk-calorie buffet, this constantly mutating strip of four-lane road is totally indistinguishable from the other four million miles of Bagley and threadbare suburban arteries just like it. I'm not saying this place or its anonymous churn from exurb to suburb to nowhere is poignant or pointless. Shit changes; you deal with it. A description this lengthy is only merited (and only to me) because this is literally where I was born.

There's one other quirk that is worth mentioning. There's a graveyard in the parking lot of the Regal Cinemas, a carpet scrap left behind when a farm or several farms got turned into a strip mall. Some of the town founders of Middleburg Heights, to the extent that a non-place needs to have founders, are buried in this plot. For some reason or another, the real estate negotiation that brought the multiplex/shopping center into the world included a deal point that these dozen or so 19th century interments had to stay put. Whenever I am confronted with the dead people in the parking lot (which is not that often), I think about the hereafter. I think about where I might go after I close my eyes for the last time. I think about some of the first people to live where I was raised, and how their bones spend eternity rattling in the dulled sonic backwash of screenings of *Transformers 3*.

I left Berea when I was 18 and have spent my entire adult life, save a few months, elsewhere. I deliberately did not apply to any colleges in the state of Ohio. I had exactly zero intention of ever moving back to Cleveland. This was in part because I was 18 and all 18-year-olds are assholes, just as a matter of brain chemistry. I didn't want to live in Cleveland, and I especially didn't want to live in the suburbs of Cleveland, because I felt that I had a total understanding of what life in Cleveland or its suburbs was or could be. I wanted no part of that life.

I don't regret leaving, because someplace else was where I found my life. I found it first in Chicago, where I lived for most of nine years, and then in New York City, where I've lived for four years. Both places are global cities, hosts to a diversity of income, origin, and taste that impoverishes the imagination. Both places make Cleveland look like a cardboard cutout. I still think of Chicago—not Cleveland—as home, even though I'm not "from" there. I am unjustly proud of my 773 area code cell phone number. I've been waiting for my Chicago-love to grow a layer of dust and eventually scuttle into deep storage in my heart, but it's a stubborn sentiment. The never-sufficiently-praised Nelson Algren famously wrote of Chicago, "Yet once you've come to be part of this particular patch, you'll never love another. Like loving a woman with a broken nose, you may well find lovelier lovelies. But never a lovely so real." Chicago is real, there's no disputing that. I do love Chicago, because it's where my real life started. As for never loving another, I'm afraid I have not been faithful.

Loving, or even just enjoying, New York is like loving a very pretty, very smart, very accomplished, independently wealthy person who just got a nose job. They were pretty before and they'll be prettier after, but they won't be the same. New York, which is made up of ugly and lovely in varying measures, is entirely unreal. I am usually misanthropic and often semi-broke, and I still cannot prevent myself from accidentally, profoundly enjoying life here. Whatever it is that someone likes, it exists in this city for the harvesting. That's not normal. New York in 2012 is a fever dream of urbanity, a cornucopia of things to consume and participate in. It is a marvel. It's so big and plural that it's nothing like a community. New York mostly exists to circulate money. The most efficient providers of said substance are tourists and the wealthy, and the camp followers of those groups. There is nothing wrong with this. It is not my idea of heaven, and at its worst, it's not that far from my idea of hell, but it is a place that historical forces and people's choices have created, just like a burning river or Chernobyl.

I stopped living in the Cleveland area 13 years ago, but I am still not free of the place, and I never will be. As much as I love Chicago and found myself there, I'm not from there. As much as I cherish my monthly MTA card and my Film Forum membership and the fact that I don't need a car, I am not from New York. I'm from Cleveland, and that's part of who I am. Even though I'm not even really from Cleveland proper, and the number of nights in my life that I've slept in the actual city of Cleveland is zero, I still can't stop feeling like I belong there. I unfortunately can't stop rooting for its sports teams, and can't stop ignoring the *Plain Dealer* just like I would if I were at home. It took leaving to understand what Cleveland was and wasn't: A real city with a real history and real people and very real problems, the opposite of a non-place. It took leaving to know what I had left.

There's a generation that's moving back to the Rust Belt, in part because living there is far cheaper and the economy is a mile-long flaming wreck on the highway, and for the non-affluent, is going to stay that way until Skynet takes over. Some people are moving home because they prioritize suburban-style consumption patterns—cars the size of condos and grills the size of cars and AC and wall-to-wall carpeting—and they can't afford to act like that in brownstone Brooklyn or Chicago's condominium reefs. Some people are coming back for jobs or culture or because having your mom and dad around suddenly seems a lot more appealing after you become a mom or dad yourself. But sneering at the reasons why people move home, how the brain drain got clogged, is just identity politics. Identity politics, especially on the topics of gentrification and the right to the city, can be wrenching. So fuck identity politics for a minute. People are moving back, and that, as a precondition for the rebirth of a real community, is the only thing that matters. I don't know if I'll ever be one of them, but I do know that 18-year-old me was a dumbass.

The Rust Belt is at once very real and something of a mirage. It took a miracle to make the factories and foundries and neighborhoods of Cleveland burst into flower, to make vibrant and meaningful cultures to spring up here, in Pittsburgh, in Buffalo, in the Mahoning Valley, in Detroit and Chicago. It took the exact opposite of that miracle to empty out those jobs and homes, to send us scurrying to the suburban desert, to very nearly forsake the idea of community. A community—what New York City can't be—is the closest thing we have to heaven. Middleburg Heights probably can't host the community I want either, although the only way to prove that would be to try to build one. Cleveland, as a place that needs and wants people, is a fallow field, desperate to be the host to a living community again. It will soon be played out once more if we treat it like we have in the past. Those are the terms of use.

Life, it has occurred me as I write, amounts to what we do on the slow walk across Bagley Road from the maternity ward to the graveyard in the parking lot. Your personal parking lot is different from mine, but in the end we're all paved over by the tides of history and change and the choices of people who come after us, and that's as it should be. We can try to turn our convenient parking back into a paradise, or we can wander in search of richer soils. Heaven may or may not be real, but we can't afford it in this life. That's what Cleveland is for.

Cleveland's Little Iraq

Huda Al-Marashi

My *husband and I moved to Cleveland* from a high rise in Queens with bewildered giddiness. In the mornings, we woke to the sounds of birds chirping. No sirens, no honks. Although the downtown was eerily quiet, traffic moved. Parking was ample, and the grocery stores' aisles were wide enough to accommodate carts with play cars attached—a dream come true for a mother of young children.

Still, I had my reservations about our new home in the Midwest. My husband and I were both the children of Iraqi immigrants. We'd moved to Cleveland for his work, and I didn't know how we'd fit into a region known for whiteness and farms. I doubted we'd find a Muslim community let alone a Middle Eastern supermarket.

It only took me one trip along Lorain Road and West 117th Street to realize how wrongly I'd assumed. Those two streets boasted more Middle Eastern supermarkets than I'd ever had access to my entire life. During my childhood in a California tourist town, we made monthly, hour-long drives to the closest Middle Eastern grocery. We came home with pounds of *halal* meat dumped into plastic bags that we then had to package and stack in the freezer. In New York, the scenario was the same, except I was the one with children underfoot as I portioned meat into freezer bags.

In Cleveland, we had a row of stores only miles from my home. Even better, the butchers prepared their *halal* meats in trays just like mainstream grocery stores. They had a *halal* deli and frozen foods, fresh pita bread, and an assortment of cheeses, *lebne*, jams, and olives. I found the convenience of it all dizzying.

As I stocked my refrigerator at home, I told my husband we could live here forever. We mused about where all these Arabs had come from and why we hadn't known there was a community here before. Maybe it was a spillover from Detroit? Maybe there were other Iraqis?

I discovered there were, in fact, many Arabs in Cleveland. At the Islamic Center of Cleveland—my first local mosque that actually looked like a mosque, complete with a gilded dome and minarets—I found so many Arabs my head spun. Jordanians, Palestinians, and Syrians, but no Iraqis.

I didn't understand why I sought out this community. I hadn't been to Iraq since 1979 when I was two years old. During that trip, my parents were interrogated so intensely at the airport, they decided Iraq was changing for the worse and that it wasn't safe to return. As a child, there had been only a handful of other Iraqi families in our seaside town, and in New York, the only foreign language I needed was the fragmented Spanish I used to communicate with my Colombian neighbors. I wished I could say that I missed speaking Arabic, but I didn't have that kind of relationship with my mother tongue. I had always been far more comfortable with English.

Still I continued to search. I heard of a Shia mosque in a converted church in Brecksville. At the start of our first Ramadan in Cleveland, we went there to break our fast. We met Iranians, Pakistanis, and Afghanis. They were warm and welcoming, but I wished I'd met some Iraqis, just a few families whose dialect reminded me of home.

On our way out, an Iranian woman told me her neighbor was Iraqi and that she planned on attending the Eid party to celebrate the end of a month of fasting. "Come," she said, "I will introduce you." Without my having to tell her, she understood what my young family needed: people who looked and sounded like our relatives, people who'd stand in as aunts and uncles, cousins, and grandparents.

At a West Side recreation center, I met Lenna, the wife of a neurologist and the mother of three children. From the first lilting, "*Hellow,*" I knew Lenna was a real Iraqi, born and raised. Rather than introduce myself as an American who could barely speak Arabic, as was my habit, I had a radical thought. *Try.*

I surprised myself. By the end of our conversation, Lenna could tell Arabic was my second language, but still she complimented me, told me how well I spoke for someone born in the US. We exchanged numbers, and she introduced me to the other Iraqi families in the area, most of whom had immigrated in the 1990s after the first Gulf War.

I had found an Iraqi community without my mother translating or obligating me, without my differentiating between native-born and American-born Iraqis. As a child, I'd drawn a line between those two communities, the Iraqis born in Iraq and those born in America. Those born abroad were my parents' friends—they loved gaudy furniture with gold trim, they arrived to everything at least an hour late, and they had little regard for posted rules (Seat belts were optional. Do Not Enter signs were mere suggestions.). I befriended their children who were like me—accent-free, style-conscious, and rule-abiding.

In the company of my new friends in Cleveland, though, I discovered how many stereotypes I'd held of my own people. My notions of Iraqis were based on a single community, most of whom had immigrated in the 1970s, and much of what I'd observed had been generational. These women, however, were my peers, with similar interests and tastes. They dreamt of HGTV homes, arrived places on time dressed in the latest styles, and even if they didn't always wear their seatbelts, at least they believed they should.

I became a full-fledged member of this new world. Now I was the one picking up the phone, inviting friends over and being invited places. We broke our fasts together during Ramadan in apartment-building party rooms. We picnicked in parks in the summer. We chatted and ate as our children played. All year long, there were social calls for deaths, hospital visits, and births that made the American in me rear her head at the endless socializing. But another part of me was proud. Every time I showed up with a cake in hand to welcome visiting relatives or to comfort those mourning a loved one was a small triumph over assimilation. My children would grow up knowing they belonged to more than just Cleveland; they were growing up as one more generation with ties to a country they'd never seen, with an understanding of the ravages of war.

From 2006 to 2009, the conditions in Iraq deteriorated, and the number of casualties rose steadily. During those years, we heard of new families arriving on a monthly, sometimes weekly basis. Most of the newcomers said the relief agencies had given them a choice of cities. Detroit, renowned for its Arab immigrant population, was full but Cleveland was open. They'd been told the winters were rough, but the price of living was reasonable. And so they came, nuclear families, extended families, and single mothers. Among them were doctors, lawyers, engineers, teachers, and business owners, willing to flounder in a new country so their children could succeed.

Whenever the local Iraqi community got word of new arrivals, we showed up with gifts in hand. In apartments scattered all over Cleveland's West Side, we heard harrowing stories brought from Iraq, of friends gone out to buy groceries and losing their lives to roadside bombs, fathers assassinated on their way to work, bodyguards shot at front doorsteps, children kidnapped on their way to school. We heard of suitcases packed haphazardly, a lifetime of belongings abandoned in houses far grander than the four walls they now called home.

These stories made the Iraq War more real to me than any of its past conflicts. I'd come of age learning about the Iran-Iraq War, the Gulf War and its sanctions by listening in on adult conversations. My siblings and I were never spoken to directly about Iraq. We were merely threatened to finish our plates with the mention of starving Iraqi children. We were told we'd have nightmares if we snuck peeks at the contraband Arabic newsmagazine circulating among my parents' friends, the one with pictures of brutally wounded child soldiers. Growing up, the only impression I had of Iraq was one of vast, blistering suffering. Those of us born in America were the guilty survivors, raised on an excess of food and American television, distant from our culture, the owners of shamefully sparse Arabic vocabularies.

But within this community, I was useful in exile for the first time. I edited the resumes and college applications of our new arrivals, wrote letters, and made calls. Someone was benefitting from my English.

There was Khawla, a striking woman in her early forties and the mother of three boys. She had been a teacher in Baghdad and the wife of an engineer. Now she was a single mother living in a Lakewood apartment. Her husband had worked at a power plant and was suspected to have been killed by insurgents with something to gain from keeping the power off. Prior to this, she'd enjoyed a comfortable life, surrounded by family and friends, never wanting for money or help with her children. She never thought one day she'd be living in America without a husband, that she'd have to support her children alone and learn a new language.

At her second-hand dining-room table, we studied together. She tutored me in Arabic, and I tutored her in English. She was sharp, a fast learner who didn't ask me to translate anything for her. She only wanted me to correct the essays she'd labored through with her "best friend," the nickname she'd given to her Arabic-English dictionary.

The afternoon her ESL teacher assigned an essay on a terrible day in your life, Khawla told me of searching for husband and winding up in the midst of a car bombing. The blast picked her up and threw her against a wall. When she came to, she was certain she was in hell. Bits of blood and flesh from the exploded bodies had burrowed into her mouth and nose and clung to her face and clothes.

"In those days," she added, "people would bring in their clotheslines and find the same kind of pieces of bodies on their clothes and sheets."

Now I was the one on the frontlines, bringing home stories to tell my parents. I told them about Khawla, about our friends who'd just gotten word of cousins who'd left Iraq for London only to be caught in a roadside bomb on their first visit home. "They said the only way they recognized them was from the pounds in their pocket." Then there was the horrific tale of the Sunni and Shia newlyweds, kidnapped on their honeymoon. Their parents got a phone call, telling them where to pick up their children. When they arrived, all they found were two bodies in garbage bags.

But as Iraq fell apart on sectarian lines, Cleveland's little Iraq fused closer together. I wasn't authentic enough to intuit from last names and cities of origin which of our friends were Sunni and which were Shia, and for our purposes, the distinction was irrelevant. Nearly half the couples we knew were of mixed sects. The eating, the visiting, and the gathering continued—an occasional engagement party, a birthday party for a family's first child born in America, a Qur'an ceremony for the deceased, a small tea party to distract someone missing a wedding back home.

My parents and their friends had spoken of the siblings' weddings they'd missed, the funerals they'd only imagined from afar. Now I was watching these emotions play out firsthand—the grief a missed happy occasion could inspire, the regret that could take mourning to excruciating heights, the nagging question of whether the costs of coming to America had been too high. Through the tears, I heard the same line over and over again, "If it was for me, I wouldn't have come, but we have to endure this for our children."

There is no word for "stress" in Arabic with the same connotation of strain on one's physical and mental well being, and so many of the newest arrivals say of the American lifestyle, "*Kulla* stress," using the English word in an otherwise Arabic sentence. They have adopted the word "busy" as well. "*Ani sayra haweya* busy," they say when they fall behind in their social calls. They say it with regret because there is a loneliness to their new lives they cannot shake.

Cleveland's Little Iraq is becoming a hybrid just like this mix of Arabic and English, just like me. Every year that passes, I watch the Iraqi children's accents drop away. They arrived not knowing more than a handful of words, but now their tongues have swallowed English, adore English, think and dream and play in English.

On New Year's Eve, we gather in the apartment of friends. One of our recent arrivals plays the guitar. I can't sing along to any of the Arabic songs our group belts out with relish.

In between songs, our hostess asks me, "Are you bored?"

Over the years, my friends have come to know the limits to my vocabulary; they can anticipate the cultural references that I will miss. They are sensitive to this, but I'm no longer. This is the gift Cleveland has given me. It has made me comfortable in my role as a translator, a bridge.

"Let's find an English song," she calls out.

Our guitarist strums the tune to "Hotel California." The lyrics leave our mouths off-key, sometimes thick and accented, but familiar to everyone.

Drinks on the River

Kristin Ohlson

The *men came every day,* arriving as the daytime manager slid back the bolt on the front door. They walked into a darkness so solid they'd tip their heads as if dodging a blow. They knew the path even in the gloom; they'd edge past the tables in the main dining room, skirt the coffee machines and pinball games in the second dining room, rap on the doors to the kitchen, glance at the shattered door to the women's bathroom, then emerge into the waterlogged light of the back bar. The Cuyahoga River was just outside, so dirty then that I washed off its spittle with soap if any happened to land on me. Marty told me that he had once seen a dead baby float by after a storm—actually, he said "dead nigger baby"—but he might have said it just to enrage me.

If the men were year-round regulars, they'd take the same places in the back bar every day. The two old guys, Manhattans at a two-top, affable big tippers; I was the highlight of their day and happy to oblige. A heavy, red-nosed salesman took the first barstool, a big-headed piece of television talent nabbed the next, and a line of businessmen from the neighborhood filled up the rest of the bar. Theirs wasn't a story-swapping, back-slapping fraternity. Aside from my two sweet old men, the back bar guys were a grim bunch who made spiritless commentary about politics and bitter jokes about women. They seemed to take little note of each other, but when one would arrive later than usual, they'd all pick up their heads and the late one would offer a quick excuse as he hoisted himself onto his stool.

Val was only a fair-weather regular, even though he worked right across the street. I think he might have come year round if it weren't for the prospect of eating lunch in that tight little room with those men who were so unlike him. He came in the spring, when the weather got warmer and the crowd spilled outside and across the deck.

Summer nights were wild. There was always a band playing in either the main room or out on the deck, and the place was packed. Many people parked cars in the big wasteland next to the railroad tracks; others plowed their boats up the river and tied them alongside the deck, sometimes five or six deep. There was lots of drinking, but little fighting; too many off-duty cops were around for a fight to build much momentum. Every once in a while, someone fell in the river. Lots of ashtrays wound up there too, as people winged them like Frisbees at the rats.

Marty and the other owners called the riverborne customers "boat pigs," but then again, there weren't many people they liked. They welcomed the back bar regulars and the off-duty cops; everyone else was tolerated as the price of doing business. Once a group of Japanese tourists came in and I heard one of the owners stomping around, muttering about the damned Nips. I called him a racist, and he drew back. "Krissie," he said in a shocked voice, "I'm not a racist. I hate everyone." Another time I failed to screw on the top of a mustard container right, and it squirted yellow goo when a customer started to fix up his hot dog. The owners went to tell the guy they'd dry clean his jacket. When they returned to the kitchen, they were furious with him for having been the victim of my error. "What did we tell you, Krissie?" they said. "The customer is always an asshole."

I have no memory of the women who came as customers, but I remember the other women who worked there. The graphic artist who served drinks in the back bar with Marty. The sweet, earnest schoolteacher on summer break who drew the adoration of one of the off-duty cops, a scary guy who wore a swastika and stormed small towns with his motorcycle pals. The multiply pierced girl, a member of Mensa, whose family had a business packaging carnival trinkets. We were intersecting each other's lives at odd points, on furlough from ordinary pursuits— school or marriage or career—and for a while I had the notion that every woman should spend some time in a job like this where the work is all restless motion, where you glance off people's lives as you bring them their beer and fries, where you walk back and forth from gloom into sunshine, where the music coming over the loudspeaker makes you dance your way to the tables, your hips jingling change, your neck and arms reflected in the tray you hold high over your head. You have secret knowledge of what the cooks are up to in the kitchen, you know what happens in the parking lot late at night, you know there are dark rooms in this building that no one imagines, but you're the emissary of good times. You smile and you flirt and you are paid.

When I first went to apply for this job, I was drawn by one of the few ads in the paper that was about something I thought I could do. My husband had just moved out of town. I was alone with my two children in the little yellow house on the west side of Cleveland, and I had no friends. It was all right. It was a new life. I was hired, spent the first few days training, and after that I was a good waitress. It had been a long time since I had been good at something.

Marty was my boss. He pointed out what needed to be done in a tone that suggested I might never catch on and that it didn't much matter anyway. There was no conversation between us. He watched my early ineptitude with what seemed like scorn, but that may have been the only way he wanted his face read. I was afraid of him at first, but got used to him after working there a few months. Then we started to fight.

We fought all the time. In his little back bar fiefdom, he and his semi-circle of soured men had something vile to say about everyone. Marty had a cartoon taped to the wall that showed a man and a woman in bed, the man saying something like, "Respect you in the morning? I don't even respect you now!" and that pretty much served as their statement of principle. When they talked about politics or city doings, they'd usually have something to say about niggers or Polacks or rednecks. Once, one of them even made some laudatory crack about Auschwitz that made me slam down a tray and walk out. I was not long out of political activism, in which I spent my days working on rent strikes or picketing grocers that sold scab grapes or demonstrating against a Cleveland cop who had gunned down a young black man. Somehow, I had wound up in the enemy camp.

But I liked the work and the grittiness of the place, the party atmosphere at night, the thrilling proximity of these off-duty cops who might once have shoved me against a wall and were now asking for extra sugar. I especially liked going at it with Marty. We'd argue up and down the halls and into the kitchen, stopping when the crowds came, continuing the conflict by facial expression alone—my sneers and his smirks—and starting up again when the customers dwindled to a handful. I was comfortable in my hatred until one morning, when I found him hosing the cups and cigarette butts and napkins from a wild Friday night into the river. I shouted that I was going to report him to the EPA. He replied without even looking up, "Oh, come on. You know you like me."

I was silenced by this, standing in the not-yet warm sun, surrounded by the smell of water on concrete and beyond that, the midsummer stench of the river. I knew it was true, but I had no idea why. Sexual attraction didn't explain it. Marty was far from the physical type that draws my eye (that's where Val comes into this story), and he wasn't even an appealing version of blond and blue-eyed. His hair was combed in sharp, aggressive angles, his eyes were small and tight, he wore the collar of his shirt turned up and always had a cocktail straw twitching at the side of his mouth. I don't think I was his type, either. Still, there was something between us, some mysterious wire of affinity.

Val became one of the regulars at the beginning of my second summer. He always came alone. He was friendly and courteous, a slight man with luminous black hair and delicate hands stained by his work. He was an artist who had turned to painting signs for a living; he liked his small simple life at home with his parents; he thought long before he answered my questions. Soon I found myself looking around for him when the place opened up for business, my blood quickening as I watched him unfold his napkin. I discovered that he was looking for me, too. I'd see him scan the deck, stare into the glassy darkness of the main room, glance into the back bar; I saw that his eyes fixed on me as I walked into the light. When I went back into the building and turned to look, I could see him watching the point of my disappearance, waiting.

This was the summer that I would turn 30, and I thought my life was breaking free of all the wrong moves of the past ten years. I told everyone that I was going back to school in the fall. I imagined that I could do it all—go to class in the day, work the river place at night. I don't know what I thought I would do with my children.

I started to see Val after work, but things didn't work out. For all his dreamy gazing at me, he seemed uncomfortable when the two of us were actually alone. After a few nights of his hesitations, I'd decide that I had misunderstood everything, but then the next day at work, he'd act as if he only came alive when I was walking across the deck. One night we went to a series of places—a park down by the river, a restaurant, a bar, a friend's apartment—then wound up back at my house wrestling around on the couch. We heard my son start to cry upstairs and broke away from each other.

My husband came back a week after that last failed date. He had become thin and sickly with misery during our separation, and he wanted me and our marriage back again. After a brief period of resistance I gave in. I gave in because of our children and our families; these were the only things I was sure of. I didn't love my husband then, although I did come to love him again later.

And I rarely think of Val now. When I decided to go back to my husband, I walked over to Val's studio and told him. I wanted him to seize my hands and cry, "No! No!" His eyes shone with what could have been tears, but he didn't try to talk me out of it. In the months after, my passion for him died away. It wasn't useful to me, and it's not even a curiosity to me now. I can remember all the things that drew me to Val—the dark eyes, the way he applied his delicate fingers to his trade, the mysterious distance—but they don't add up to a feeling.

But I still think about Marty. I'm reminded of him whenever I see men glower around a bar. I think about him when I go out to eat or drink—despite the smiling hostess, I know that the cooks might be cursing the food, the bartenders breathing dismay into the drinks. I know that the unlikeliest of people can get in the people business. There's a blues club downtown and years later someone told me that Marty was working there. I stopped once and asked about him and left my name. I went again a few months later and the bartender told me he had moved on. He drew a little map on a napkin for me, but by the time I found the place Marty was supposed to be working, it had closed.

Why did I look for him? It's common enough to fall in and out of love with someone—I do it all the time—but to like and be liked by someone you hate on principle is an enduring wonder. I still get a thrill thinking about that place by the river: the off-duty cops shooting rats in the parking lot, the cooks sweating and singing and flinging burned shrimp at the wall. Marty and me. All our magnificent glares.

The Long, Slow Walk of Detroit Shoreway

Lee Chilcote

S*oon after my wife and I moved* to the Cleveland EcoVillage in 2006, I started walking to work each day through the narrow, tree-lined streets of the West Side.

It was a 20-minute walk from our townhouse to the real-estate company where I worked. On the way, I passed a Gothic stone church, a community garden where corn and peppers burst up next to workers cottages and six or seven boarded-up homes nestled against pockets of new housing.

My commute was about a mile. If it was nice out, I dawdled a bit, checking out how the veggies were growing in the gardens or the frilly details of timeworn Victorians. In the winter, I walked a little faster to stay warm. I tried to avoid looking at my phone—my walk was a respite from the wired world, a chance look at my surroundings.

One morning, as I was walking along Ithaca Court through the EcoVillage garden, I got a call on my cell phone and decided to pick it up. Distracted, I failed to notice someone trying to talk to me. I saw an elderly man leaning out of the doorway of his tiny home, a cottage with warped gutters and flaking paint at the edge of the garden.

We exchanged pleasantries. He asked me who my friend was. I didn't know what he was talking about. Then I realized that he couldn't see the phone pressed to my ear, that he was blind, and that he thought I was talking to someone walking with me. I laughed and explained that I was talking on a cell phone.

As I said goodbye to Joe—we talked more, and he told me his name—a familiar feeling surfaced within me. I was a newbie in a neighborhood whose roots ran one-and-a-half centuries deep. Yes, I lived in the Cleveland EcoVillage, but I was part of a larger, older village built by immigrants. St. Stephen's, the church I passed each day, was built by German workers who moved to the neighborhood in the 1860s.

The German workers are gone, and I have watched my neighborhood change in the few years since I moved here in July 2006. That September, a year before the foreclosure crisis hit the rest of the US, I noticed changes. The up-and-down double that had always had a tricycle in the yard was suddenly empty and boarded up. The ragged four-unit where the people were always fighting was suddenly too quiet.

As we watched our neighborhood fill up with empty homes that were soon looted of copper pipes and siding, my wife and I wondered if we'd made the right choice by buying a house here. We couldn't sell our house now and didn't want to, though, so we decided to tough it out. Still, it was a rude awakening to see so much recent investment unravel so quickly.

But I saw other changes, too. In 2007, a new coffee shop opened up about a half mile from our house. It became a community gathering place where people brought their families and dogs. The owner of the shop got to know us all, and renovated the empty storefront herself. Because she'd always loved to travel, she called it Gypsy Beans and Baking Company.

We understood that we were living in a city where everything all around us was dying and being born at the same time. It was brutally disfigured by history, neglect and forces we couldn't understand, but it was ours and we wanted to believe we could reshape it.

Sometimes, when I was out walking, the layers of history I saw reminded me of the flyers that you would have found stapled to telephone poles in the '80s, advertising bands or babysitters. Peel back the top leaf—and there would be the detritus of old, hand-scrawled bulletins, like the cobblestone streets visible beneath the pavement when the snow melted in the spring.

There is something lovely about so much faded urgency, and I continue to walk the streets of Detroit Shoreway looking for signs of the neighborhood's past and future.

tins, like the cobblestone streets visible beneath the pavement when the snow melted in the spring.

There is something lovely about so much faded urgency, and I continue to walk the streets of Detroit Shoreway looking for signs of the neighborhood's past and future.

Slavic Village Deli

Erin O'Brien

The *Fleet Avenue neighborhood* in Slavic Village was one of the first places all the national news shows flashed on the screen, along with words like *subprime* and *meltdown* and *crisis*, way before the rest of the country got preoccupied with the words *Great Recession*. They showed the mainly empty streets with a few houses remaining, looking like the mouth of a kid who just lost a bunch of teeth. Slavic Village was "ground zero" of the housing crisis, and thousands of houses have since been torn down on account of that being a better option than leaving them vacant.

But sometimes our heart beats strongest where our fabric is worn thinnest, and while this neighborhood may be torn and frayed, the Slavic Village Deli remains.

When you enter, the first thing you see is the take-out counter. Old school from the bottom up. Homemade Polish sausages and baked goods. The pretty girl with the Polish accent and the apron hanging around her hips in a way that makes boys swoon will wrap up all your stuff in white paper so perfectly she'll make you weep.

Up and down the wall are narrow shelves crammed with jars and cans arranged just so. I don't know why canned stuff imported from Europe somehow looks better than regular canned stuff at the Giant Eagle. And no, I don't know what any of it is. But I always buy some anyway, along with a sack full foil-wrapped confections.

In the back is the dining room. There they serve low-cooked kielbasa and sauerkraut, cabbage and noodles, homemade mashed potato and stuffed cabbage, just like the men in coveralls and heavy work shoes carried in their lunch pails as they trudged to the steel mills every morning. And for dessert? Butter cookies or a square of poppy seed pound cake.

Now, I'm not trying to freak you out or anything, but sometimes when you eat those potato pancakes you feel like your shoulder blades are unfurling into feathered wings. Don't worry. It's not too painful. You're in Slavic Village, after all. You can take the hurt.

Little Italy's Shabby Chic

Clare Malone

I *came to the conclusion* early on in life that Italians know how to do things up right.

It was not a fabulous family vacation to Rome or Tuscany that put this notion into my head—our trips were strictly confined to Civil War battlefields and glamorous locales like Catawba, New York—nor was it any kind of inherited family pride—I come from a long line of Sullivans, Brennans, McNallys, and Malones who have been and always will be as pale as the Etruscans are olive-skinned. No, it was Murray Hill (right where it intersects with Mayfield Road), not the Capitoline Hill, that set my heart aflutter. I was in love with Little Italy the moment I laid eyes on it, and still am, though it's a long-distance thing now, with me pining away from the East Coast.

A lot this love initially had to do with the fact that I was a kid who liked to eat. Sure, Geraci's pizza was all right, but their sweet tomato sauce was the happy stuff of the Heights. Pies from Mama Santa's, served under low, slightly seedy lighting that bounced off plastic tablecloths and fake mahogany walls, were true Sicilian magic. They weren't the prettiest slices, the kind that are drizzled with fresh olive oil and were topped with a shapely basil leaf, but damn, that pizza was good.

And of course there were Presti's donuts, succulent little creatures that I credit for edging me up a couple weight percentiles the summer before fifth grade. My sisters and I took art classes at University

Circle, and almost every afternoon, we begged for a treat from the shop. To this day, sweets that hemorrhage jelly and custard take me back to those sun-dappled afternoons and my ample 10-year-old thighs.

But the food was just the beginning. Though Little Italy was only 15 minutes from my house at the border of Shaker Heights and Beachwood, it wasn't just the elevation that changed as you drove down Edgehill Road from the Heights. Passing by the double houses festooned with Italian flags and statues of the Virgin Mary, riding along on the uneven brick road—it all transported you into the Cleveland of your parents' and grandparents' stories. I could practically picture the Holy Rosary boys biking up the hill to rumble with the St. Anne's crew, straight from my father's preadolescent parish-rivalry lore.

The neighborhood was cozy—small, tended yards and porches—but also citified, with coin laundry storefronts and windowless drinking establishments. Achingly beautiful old buildings stood next to unimpressive utilitarian structures; there were shops where you could buy art—for a while Omar Vizquel even sold his paintings in one—and kitschy places for knick-knacks, my favorite of which we dubbed "The Frank Sinatra Store" for the simple reason that the proprietors blasted a constant soundtrack of Ol' Blue Eyes. They carried tulle-laden first communion dresses and zebra-striped jewelry; the saleswomen always wore rhinestones, it seemed. Outside, two or three old men stood around smoking.

Even going to Mass in Little Italy was better; the altarpiece at Holy Rosary looked like something from a museum Christmas card, with a starry sky, the Madonna, and hosts of angels. Plus, the statues were done in what appeared to be Technicolor, a paint-on-plaster technique that had long since passed out of fashion at our staid, lace-curtain Irish parish.

By the time I hit high school, I realized that Little Italy was imbued with the kind of shabby-chic glamour beloved by Hollywood screenwriters and whoever puts together Martha Stewart's cookbooks. My friends and I started going to La Dolce Vita's Tuesday Ladies' Night; $10 for pasta and a drink, and an occasion to wear high heels and eye makeup. The place was pitch-perfect, with tomatoes and fat candles sitting on wrought-iron candelabras, Italian movies screening on the walls, and a minimalist interior. I'm fairly certain it's where I learned how to honest-to-goodness flirt. We were rewarded for my efforts with a complimentary dessert of Grand Marnier-soaked fruit from our waiter, and the knowledge that all young girls really do have their charms.

I moved away from Cleveland for college with what I can only describe as a fierce wanderlust coupled with a deep desire to wear whimsical sundresses 24/7. But I wanted to bottle that intoxicating feeling I got when sitting at a tiny café table in Little Italy, eating off white china, while Frank Sinatra and cigarette smoke wafted in the background. I figured the cities of the Eastern Seaboard could help me out with that. Four years later, I moved even farther away—about 8,000 miles—to live in a desert country I'd never even heard of when I was 17 and wearing my sister's lipstick and sipping a Diet Coke on a Little Italy sidewalk.

"How are you going to get them back to the farm once they've seen the big city?" my mother has exclaimed to me on more than one occasion. I'm back living on the East Coast again and think of this often—guiltily—though never without my mind tumbling into another one of her perhaps-truisms, that Midwestern and Rust Belt kids are the bravest. Their cities are not the cities that are lauded for being the crown jewels of a civilization. The Rust Belt kid grows up and sees sputtering steel mills, abandoned lots, masterpieces in the art museum, and the tidy yards of slightly frayed yet still-stately homes lining wide boulevards. What she means is, they know the scope of what there was and is, so they figure they've got nothing to lose by trying to go find the "could be again" in a place far from home. That's a mother's love, conjuring up a theory of bravery to ease a child's guilt for an act of abandonment.

Little Italy is still something rich and strange to me, with all the jumbled romance of city living. I've even noticed a new charm to it. On the corner where Murray Hill and Mayfield Roads meet, there's an old red brick building with a small turret at the top. "What a perch that would be," I think when I pass by now, with Frank Sinatra, cigarette smoke, and a real city view to keep you company. I just don't know if I'm brave enough to deserve it quite yet.

III. History

Bob Perkowski

Unstoppable Houses On Changeless Terrain

Michael Ruhlman

Buildings matter. And the terrain on which those buildings rise matters. The shape of the terrain, unlike razable buildings, doesn't change. The slope of the land helps one to understand a city's development. I can begin to walk, for instance, at the northernmost oxbow of the crooked river, near where the boy John Rockefeller had his first offices, on Superior in the Flats. It's a hill. You have to lean forward to climb it, but it's short, and as the land levels out, it's a few minutes' walk straight ahead to the town center called, earnestly, Public Square, anchored by the Terminal Tower. There's a reason for its distance from the river. You wouldn't build a square on the river or on a hill: a good square needs plenty of space all around it, but you'd also want it not too far from the river. It had been placed just right, a quarter mile or so from the bustling river commerce, and it had been especially accommodating when its pastoral warmth had a community feel to it, a wide dirt road surrounding four grassy, stump-and-tree-filled quadrants. I'd have paid as much attention then to a wild swine crossing my path as I would a squirrel today. Cows got in there to graze, which annoyed people. In the summertime the air would be redolent of horse manure and dirt; in the winter you'd want a really good pair of boots just to cross the street.

As I approach, the massive brick monolith built by Standard Oil of Ohio—now owned by the British Petroleum Company and referred to as the BP building—looms over the square, but the square's oldest buildings remain, hinting at its original grandeur. On the north side is the Old Stone Church, dedicated there in 1834, razed and rebuilt in 1853 in Romanesque Revival Style, its blackened stones a pleasure to behold. The building across the street, the Society for Savings Building, completed in 1890, is composed of huge blocks of red sandstone, more gorgeous today than they would have been then, when such material was commonplace.

I could walk east from the foot of the British Petroleum Building along Euclid Avenue to East 40th Street to know just how long Flagler and Rockefeller would have had to plan and plot their rebate deal and their Standard Oil trust as they walked to and from work, a route they traveled four times daily, a distance less than two miles.

Rockefeller's house had been torn down decades ago, and a gas station, appropriately enough, went up in its place, though even that's gone now. One of the two remaining Millionaires' Row mansions, now a CSU administrative building, sits above an overpass, endless cars zipping by on Interstate 90—a dowager looking down upon the future.

Euclid Avenue itself was likely created by the tread of the feet of Native Americans, a path once called the Buffalo Road because that was how you got to Buffalo, New York, 180 miles away. The path became a dirt road. It widened, and people built houses on it. They put planks down on it to make travel in wet seasons easier. They had sleigh races during the winter, the competitors bundled in coats made from buffalo hides. Soon the city paved the street.

Foot tread had designed the main transportation route east out of the city, the route along which John Hartness Brown, a Cleveland businessman, took Patrick Calhoun during the summer of 1890, an event that began the neighborhood in which our house sits. Mr. Brown would have used an actual carriage hitched to a couple of horses and likely picked up Calhoun in the hot, dusty bustle of Public Square, industrial smoke rising out of the Flats and into the sky. The day was likely warm, and the city's center teemed with horses and bicycles and horse-drawn streetcars kicking up dust. Shoppers along Superior tied their mounts to wooden posts outside stores. Ladies wore bustles and kept the sun off their pale necks with parasols. Men wore collars and hats despite the heat of a clear summer day.

Calhoun, the grandson of statesman and politician John Calhoun, was a tall, commanding, and self-assured railroad lawyer and en-
trepreneur from South Carolina. He had short fair hair and vivid blue
eyes in a round face. He read the Stoic philosophers and took icy baths in
the morning. He had a temper, was stern and aggressive to the point of
arrogance but also charismatic. A year before this trip, he'd challenged to
a duel a fellow Atlanta lawyer who'd impugned his character; both men
emerged unscathed and good friends. He was devoted to his wife and
eight children.

Having concluded his railroad business—he'd traveled here to
increase railroad commerce between the busy center of Cleveland and
South Carolina—and with his own train not departing till evening, Calhoun took a ride east with Mr. Brown to see the Garfield Monument, a
180-foot Byzantine-Gothic structure, apparently the first true American
mausoleum, serving as both tomb and memorial for the country's 20th
president, and dedicated just a few months earlier.

In a few minutes' time, Brown could have pointed to his right at
Rockefeller's understated Euclid Avenue house. Rockefeller was in town
that month enjoying Forest Hills (he wouldn't buy his Pocantico Hills
estate in New York for three more years). Indeed, Rockefeller may well
have been the one who put Calhoun up to this in the first place. Brown
might then have notes that there, on their left as they approached the
bustling Doan's Corners, was the residence of Dr. Worthy Streator, a
landowner active in many of the city's industries and railroads.

While along Millionaires' Row, they would have enjoyed a peace-
ful ride on their fine summer day, but after Doan's Corners, a thriving
commercial center, Brown and Calhoun would have crossed a streetcar
line at Wade Park.

According to Calhoun's son-in-law, Warren Wick, who'd grown
up on Millionaires' Row, the member of a prominent banking family,
Calhoun at this point said to Brown, "Where does Cleveland grow from
here? I haven't seen a vacant property all the way out Euclid Avenue."

Brown intended to show Calhoun and took him the back way, up
a winding dirt road called Cedar Glen. The horse and carriage and the
summer birdsong would have been the only sounds, along with perhaps
the gobbling of turkeys crossing the road or the cart of one of the Gyp-
sies who squatted around here heading down to trade at Doan's Corners.

Cedar Glen was heavily forested with alder, oak, maple, and elm, and so they rode in shade. The going would have been relatively smooth on a dry day along this half-mile bend, a bank rising to 275 feet above lake level.

When they crested the top of the hill, Calhoun beheld a rolling plateau of cleared land, used now for cattle and horses, and, farther east, vineyards and rock quarries. It was a lovely pastoral vista, refreshing after the hot, dusty Public Square, where his journey began.

They proceeded north toward the monument, its spire visible in the distance below. Calhoun and Brown gazed at Lake Erie spreading out, three miles off and in clear view. Turning to their left, they could see oil-refinery and steel-mill smoke. Rising out of the city to these heights to behold this vista clearly had a dramatic effect on Calhoun. He must have sensed he'd arrived on this plateau at an unusually auspicious moment. He had just come from Richmond, Virginia, where innovative city developers were for the first time linking electric street railways, new technology, with residential real estate development. The United States was flush with cash; industry thrived. Here he saw undeveloped land near a booming industrial city, tenth biggest in the country and growing.

This essay is excerpted from Michael Ruhlman's memoir House

Tales of the Regional Art Terrorists

David C. Barnett

T *he lips are gone.* For years, they floated on an abutment at the base of the Detroit-Superior bridge in the Flats: a big pair of shiny red-enamel lips framing a mouthful of teeth. It was a Cheshire grin that greeted patrons stumbling out of the old Flat Iron Cafe. The lips first appeared sometime in the late 1970s, covering up an obscene tag someone had scrawled on the wall with an aerosol paint can. Below the lips was an equally mysterious signature announcing that this graffiti was the work of some so-called "Regional Art Terrorists."

"Terrorist" spokeswoman May Midwest told a *Cleveland Press* reporter in 1979 that the group was about 300 strong and had been responsible for other aesthetic attacks, including huge strands of silver Mylar that showed up one morning, wafting from the girders of the same bridge. And then there was the billboard on Mayfield Road near Little Italy, which featured the TV-8 news anchor team. The Regional Art Terrorists had added sunglasses to each face, and beneath the sign's request to "GET TO KNOW US BETTER" was the handwritten counter-suggestion: "IGNORE ALIEN ORDERS."

Well-known Cleveland gallery owner William Busta was never an art terrorist, but admits he certainly sympathized with them. "I think we all felt a little bit marginalized by the city," he says, "but we also cared very deeply about the city—maybe more than a lot of the people who ran it. At that time, there were even some Cleveland City councilmen who actually lived in the suburbs."

Busta himself was a product of the suburbs, but as a young person, he felt the pull of downtown. "When you told your parents that you were getting an apartment in Cleveland, your parents and everybody you knew looked at you as if you were crazy and discouraged it."

"May Midwest" was the pseudonym of a young art student named Melissa Craig who was pretty much the leader of this renegade band of 20-something artists. Lips were her graphic trademark. They showed up in cartoons she wrote for alternative weeklies, in commercial illustrations she did for local bands, and in her own more serious work.

Craig's comic strips were populated by assorted talking hamburgers, rats, chickens, and vegetables making off-the-wall commentaries about urban life. Always lurking among this cosmopolitan crowd was a resigned and slightly sad-looking female character with a radioactive hairdo. It brings to mind Melissa Craig's weirdly colored hair when she was a 13-year-old runaway in the mid-1960s. She'd had a bad run-in with a bottle of peroxide in an attempt to disguise her identity from county authorities. Craig laughs at the memory of those early years: "The only thing close to it was David Bowie. I didn't look like myself anymore, but in 1964 I looked a little strange. Plus, the only clothes I had were a neon-orange shirt and black pants."

Craig says she became so well known around the juvenile detention home that the matrons nicknamed her "Neapolitan", after her distinct hairstyle. She spent most of her early teen years alternating between the detention facility, foster homes, and the street. For a two-month period, she and two friends lived in the cavernous women's washroom in the bowels of the Terminal Tower, sleeping in the stalls between cleaning shifts.

By the time she was 15, Craig started getting waitress jobs on and off. A slight detour with a male companion took her to Rapid City, S.D., for three years, where she continued waitressing, but started drawing caricatures of her friends on the side. "I always knew I wanted to be an artist," she recalls, "I just forgot it for a while, trying to live."

Longtime friend Bill Busta says that was the start of a long and distinguished artistic career for Melissa Craig. "She really grew up on the streets of Cleveland. By her own scrappiness and her intelligence, and with a brave and strong heart, she created a whole life for herself. She had no access to anything. She had to create a lot of things from scratch."

Steven Smith is another close friend of Craig, and is himself something of an underground legend in the Cleveland art scene since the late 1970s. For twenty years, his publication, *Art Crimes*, was a compendium of the region's major poets, painters, and collage artists. Smith met Melissa Craig at an art show and they became fast friends.

"Melissa is the most talented person I know, across categories," he says. "I mean, most visual artists are bad with words. She's good with words, she's good with painting, she's good with sculpture, and as a teacher—she's just good with everything she does."

Both Smith and Craig were part of an itinerant group of artists who moved around Cleveland in search of cheap rents in abandoned neighborhoods. Craig had a loft space in the Flats, and Smith was a pioneer in the Warehouse District, when it was truly a district of warehouses.

"I was paying $300 a month for 3,000 square feet on the fourth floor," he recalls. "I had four windows overlooking the lake. I had nine windows overlooking Cleveland. I stayed there five years."

It was a spartan existence. You entered through a 15-by-25-foot fire door into a room with 20-foot ceilings. There was a toilet, a work sink, and a previous occupant had put in a fiberglass shower. Smith and his friends hauled in a refrigerator and a stove and created a kitchen. The rest of the place was filled with art, parties, and philosophical discussions into the night. He smiles at the memory. "I had always admired Hemingway in 1920s Paris. Well, the Warehouse District was my 'Hemingway in Paris' era."

That era came to an end when city officials learned he was living in a space that was zoned for commercial activity. Years later, those zoning restrictions were lifted, and the neighborhood became a hotbed for young urban professionals looking for a unique address near their downtown offices.

Steven Smith moved to what was then a different, low-rent neighborhood: Tremont. And the pattern was the same—the artists were the pioneers, followed by people with higher incomes who, to this day, continue to move into the community's growing number of condos.

Smith was also an occasional member of the Regional Art Terrorists, and he has fond memories of one of their most enduring and most dangerous escapades. Commuters on the rapid transit line coming into Cleveland from the East Side can still see remnants of this daring art attack. If you look carefully as the train is about to enter the Tower City station, you'll see the worn remains of a mural, done in the style of Egyptian temple paintings, depicting a line of commuters from another era, bearing briefcases and heading to work.

The large mural was designed to be started and completed between two trains passing by that spot along the tracks late at night. It was executed with stencils in 15 minutes and has lasted for decades.

"It's been 30 years," says Smith, "and no official has taken it off, and no other graffiti artist has tagged it. That's respect."

Melissa Craig eventually left Cleveland for Chicago where she earned an MFA and now teaches. She returns occasionally to exhibit her work, and to conduct workshops at the Morgan Conservatory—a local organization devoted to the art of papermaking.

The iconic lips that Craig painted at the base of a Flats bridge were maintained for years by others who would touch them up occasionally. But eventually, they were obliterated by a coat of gray paint intended to "clean up" the area of copious graffiti.

Lips continue to be a primal image for Melissa Craig, but these days they represent the way she understands other people. For a number of years, she has been losing her ability to hear, and today she is just about totally deaf. Ever the scrappy survivor, Craig has become quite adept at reading lips. And she still thinks a lot about her hometown—a place that she continues to love, despite some mixed feelings. After a rough life, she says she's finally found herself, but she thinks Cleveland remains saddled with some identity problems. She still has a message for the city, but this one she speaks with her own lips:

I say: be proud of what you are, while acknowledging what you were. Above all, listen to your artists, your musicians, and the other creative people who call you home. Cleveland needs to celebrate its authenticity and invest in and support what is already here, in place—from the odd, gritty beauty of its industrial heritage, to its lush vegetation to, above all, its people. Cleveland isn't anything but Cleveland, but that's all it really needs to be.

Ward 6

Jim Rokakis

June 1977. My first official campaign stop was at Merryman's Hall: a tired, two-story red brick building located at the corner of West 14th Street and Denison Ave. The club was nothing more than a small bar and ten tables. No food. Just cheap booze. Once a club for the Polish immigrants, it had now become a hangout for the sons and grandsons of the founders, but also for Appalachians who had worked their way north for the jobs at the mills and plants. The most recent wave of immigrants to the neighborhood, the Puerto Ricans, were not welcome here—not yet, anyway. When the membership rolls dropped to levels so low that the club could not pay the light bills, the membership criteria were loosened so anybody could join, as long as you had cash.

I had my one and only campaign staffer with me that night: Dave Krischer of Skokie, Ill. Dave was a junior at Oberlin College. I can't think of anyone who had less in common with the average Ward Six resident. He was Jewish. In fact, next to black people, Jews were probably the least favorite ethnic group in that neighborhood. Dave knew this. In fact he had some fun with it when the topic came up. "You a Greek like Rokakis?" I once heard him being asked. "Oh no," he'd reply. "I'm Russian. My ancestors were from Pogrom, Russia." I don't think anybody ever caught on.

The steps leading up to the hall on the second floor were long and narrow. Like every other public space in the neighborhood, the most overwhelming feature of the room was smoke. There were about 50 people in the room. At 22 years of age, I was the youngest by about 20 years. When I entered, it got quiet, heads turned. I got anxious. My throat dried.

I stopped at the sign-in table and let them know that I wanted to speak that night. The club secretary asked if I wanted to join their organization.

"Yes," I said, and gave her three bucks.

She asked if I had a door prize.

"Of course," I replied and handed her a bottle of wine I brought, complete with a tag that read "Compliments of Jim Rokakis." I forgot who told me to do that. I would like to thank them anyway. The sentiment was a lesson that would guide me through Cleveland politics for the next 30 years.

The meeting began like all meetings did in the neighborhood: with the Pledge of Allegiance. After the reading of minutes, the club president suddenly turned to me, saying: "We have a special guest here tonight, a young man named Jim Rokakis. It says here on the sign-in sheet that he is running for City Council here in Ward Six. He wants to say a few words to us."

Oh shit, I thought to myself. I felt I was going to get sick. I got up. "Thank you for the chance to speak with you this evening," I stumbled. "My name is Jim Rokakis. I'm one of your neighbors—I live on Garden Ave. I am here to announce to you that I am running for Cleveland City Council here in Ward Six. I have lived in this neighborhood all of my life, but I am unhappy with the direction that it is taking."

I continued, my tone as about as deliberate as the sound of tip-toeing: "I am really unhappy with the crime problem in this neighborhood—"

Just then I was cut off. There was a voice in the hallway, shouting: "I'm coming up. I'm coming up. Coming up babies, don't nobody come down the stairs—Sophie's coming up!"

Peals of laughter rippled throughout the room. Heads turned toward the doorway to see an enormous woman named Sophie enter. She wore a billowing white dress that was sleeveless and exposed big white arms. Her legs were trunks right down to the feet.

"Hi'ya Sophie!" somebody shouted. "Come over here, we saved a seat for you!"

She slowly worked her way over to a wooden folding chair. She sat. I stared at the chair, worried about its integrity. Sophie glared in my direction. My concentration was shot. I tried to pick up where I left off.

"People just don't feel safe anymore in this neighborhood. As I go door to door I hear stories of break-ins, cars being stolen—"

I was cut off again by a man in the front row. "I caught a nigger in my driveway last week," he began. I was floored. The man went on, "I asked him what he was doing, said he was looking for somebody named Maurice, you know that was bullshit. He was looking for a house to break into."

I turned to the club president, hoping that he would rule the man out of order for his racist remarks. Wrong. Instead he picked up the conversation where the bigot in the front row left off.

"What day did you see him? Was it Monday or Tuesday?"

"I'm sure it was Monday because I was off that day."

"Was he with anybody? Because I saw two of 'em in a station wagon, cruising and looking up and down driveways."

The conversation went on for another couple of minutes with people in the room joining in. Then someone raised their hand, pointed to me, and the club president apologized and asked me to continue. I didn't get far.

Rita LaQuatra raised her hand and asked: "Mr. Rokakis, what's better—governor or senator?"

I didn't get the question, so I asked to her to repeat it.

"I said, what's better, governor or senator?"

I stammered. "Well, they are very different jobs—both important but very different." I then ventured into the differences between the legislative and executive branches of government. After about three minutes, folks weren't paying attention. I then struggled to get back to my prepared speech.

At this point Howard Lorman of Library Avenue got up and turned to face the audience. Mr. Lorman was in his early eighties, rail thin, neatly dressed. He didn't live in that neighborhood but somewhere along the way he found this group, or they found him—or they found each other more likely.

"I would like to say something about voting," he said. "It was 1932. We use to vote in those metal sheds. Do you remember those metal sheds?"

People nodded in the smoke.

"Well, it was the primary. I asked for my ballot and looked for the name of Herbert Hoover, but couldn't find it. They told me I had asked for the wrong ballot and wouldn't give me another one. You know what I did? I wrote in the name of Adolf Hitler."

The room burst into laughter. Not long after the crowd quieted, I thanked them for the opportunity and sat down. I was drenched in sweat. I had been speaking for forty-five minutes, and it seemed I had gotten nothing across. I was disappointed. I lost control of the group early and never regained their attention.

But the evening was not a total loss. I learned a valuable lesson about neighborhood politics: Expect the unexpected. This lesson was reinforced by the fact that Ted Sliwa, the incumbent Ward 6 Councilman and a legend in Cleveland politics, would be a no-show that night, as he was all summer. I thought it was because he was confident and secure in his position. Only later did we learn that he had had it with local politics.

I consider that evening at Merryman's—my first public appearance—the night in which I was thrown to the wolves. But as difficult as the evening seemed, it paled in comparison to the experiences awaiting me less than a year away as a member of Cleveland City Council. They were the beginning of the most tumultuous two years in the city's history—Dennis Kucinich's short-lived tenure as mayor. The time would also present me with one of the toughest days I ever had in public life.

When Sliwa dropped out of the race, I became the front-runner. That much was clear. Our youth and enthusiasm had created "buzz" in the neighborhood. One problem: money wasn't coming in. Campaigns cost money, and I was broke, as were my folks. A fundraiser was needed.

My first fundraiser was a "Greek" affair at the UAW Hall on Chevrolet Boulevard in Parma. We had a Greek band, the Pyros Brothers, and Greek food. The event raised a few grand, but it only lasted us until July, and we thought maybe we'd go bigger with a neighborhood event. So we hosted a beer-and-sausage event at the VFW hall at West 49th and Memphis. I was worried it would be a bust, but also hopeful that my relentless door-to-door campaigning would somehow pay off.

Rick Morgan, my right-hand man at the time, printed up some cheap fliers and delivered them door-to-door. We had hoped for 100-

125 people. A day before the event, a man named Chuck Sayre, whom I had met on the campaign trail, asked if he could provide the evening's entertainment. Chuck was a blue-collar guy: a former boxer, then a fight promoter, then an organizer of third-rate musical acts. Talk about Rust Belt Chic, well, Chuck was it.

The night of the fundraiser came. I was petrified I would arrive to an almost empty hall. I had spent the entire day campaigning and had gone home to shower. Around 7:30, the phone rang. It was Rick, and I could barely hear him. "You better get up here," he shouted. "The crowd is huge and they are asking about you." I was stunned. I headed over to the hall immediately.

When I got the parking lot, I was shocked to see cars overflowing. Adrenaline rushed. I parked a block over and ran into the hall. As I worked my way to the door, people began to shout out my name, "Jim," "Jim, how ya doing," and "Jim, good luck!" I was shaking hands. Hugging and kissing old ladies. Smoke filled the room. Drinks flowed. In the back, Chuck had a microphone and was introducing one of his acts—an Elvis impersonator in a sequined suit—to the crowd. "Hound Dog" played and ended. Chuck then took the mic from Elvis's hand and said: "Ladies and gentlemen, the man we all been waitin' for. The guest of honor: JIMMY ROKAKIS!"

The crowd erupted. It felt like a dream. I worked my way to the head of the room and took the mic. I don't remember what I said. But I do remember closing with a question: "Are you with me?" The crowd roared yes.

To say that I expected to be a politician growing up wouldn't be the truth. The streets of my neighborhood weren't particularly nice. They weren't as tough on the Near West Side or East Side of the city, but as the years passed it was safe to say most of my neighbors were not there by choice. In fact, growing up I didn't so much focus on how to lead as much as I did on where I didn't want to follow. So much youth around me was doing time, and dying young. Like Jerry Wallace: the best athlete in the neighborhood died of cirrhosis of the liver at 30. Luckily, my family and my drive kept me away from being on the terribly wrong side of life. And so the neighborhood that grew me eventually became the neighborhood that voted me to the forefront when it was their time to be represented.

But politics is not just about public recognition; it is also about public pain, and I learned this early with the murder of an 11-year-old girl named Maxine Penner not a half year into my first term. I was sick when I got the news. I remember meeting her and her mother, Ruth Penner. They lived in a small frame house directly across from Riverside Cemetery. The media was all over this tragedy. The headlines blared: "Young girl murdered on the West Side."

I remember going to a meeting with a group of neighbors the night after the murder. They were angry. They were scared. The meeting was about ten doors away from the murder scene. I could barely look at the house where it happened when I drove by. The lights were on. The shades were drawn.

Nobody greeted me when I entered the home where the meeting was taking place. No handshakes. No smiles. The anger was thick. I remember a large heavyset man standing in the corner who charged at me, coming within inches of my face and screaming, "You ain't done shit in this neighborhood. This neighborhood has gone to hell since you became councilman!" There were shouts of approval from others in the crowd. I remember thinking this was a verbal assault I would have to take. I had no choice. I represented authority and order. And what occurred was the opposite of that: horror, disorder. When I finally responded I was brief. I told them that I would work day and night to make sure the killer(s) were caught. I reminded them that I lived in the neighborhood and shared their risk. I promised a greater police presence. I asked them to share any information—to work with me even if they didn't care for me. I asked them to say a prayer for Maxine. I stayed until almost midnight. It was and still is my hardest day in public life.

The next morning, I compiled a list of potential suspects based on what I knew of neighborhood problems and what the neighbors shared with me. The neighborhood didn't have a gang problem in the classic sense. Just a bunch of mean, hardscrabble kids from the lower West Side: Hispanic, Appalachian, and first-generation ethnics. Most abused drugs and had done time in some JV facility for relatively minor offenses. This murder was something else. And if they were the perpetrators, they had grown up: they were killers now.

I submitted the list to homicide detectives that morning and they politely accepted it. But they didn't have much to say. It was too early in their investigation. They became annoyed over the course of the next few weeks as I pressed them for answers. These weren't the days of crime labs and DNA analysis. The investigations were methodical, slow. I was afraid that they would never make an arrest.

The evening of the visitation I became sick and vomited just before I left. I knew the job of councilman wouldn't be easy, but dealing with the murder of a young girl was something else. When I went to the funeral home, I was scared I'd become emotional when I'd meet Mrs. Penner: not exactly the image of a strong leader I was meant to project. I knew I had to keep my emotions in check.

The funeral home was crowded. The people parted for me as I walked to the mother of the victim. I remember holding her and the two of us walking to the casket, where Maxine lay. The casket was open and I remember her saying something about how they had done a good covering the cuts on her neck. That's all I remember. I didn't cry. I went directly to my car and headed south on Pearl Road into Parma, Parma Heights, and then all the way into Medina County. I turned around and it was dark when I got back. I stopped at my parents' house on Garden Avenue before I returned to my empty apartment. I took an aluminum folding chair from the porch out to the backyard where I had grown up. I sat alone listening to the sounds of the neighborhood: the barking dogs, the television sets, the country music, and I cried.

A couple of months later, one of the boys on our list admitted to a juvenile detention counselor that he had some information on the murder. They arrested Curtis Richmond and charged him with rape and aggravated murder, though he served less than eight years after being allowed to plead down to manslaughter. Other juveniles admitted to being accomplices but didn't serve much time. They all said it was a botched break-in and panicked and killed her. Shortly after the funeral, Mrs. Penner left Cleveland and I never saw her again.

Maxine would be forty-six years old if she were alive today. I have not forgotten her. I never will.

Rockefeller and Rust Belt Romance

Mandy Metcalf

O ne summer, a friend invited me to the park to play sand volleyball at Whiskey Island, then a hidden park, and I married him there a few years later in the shadow of the abandoned Coast Guard station. It's a very romantic spot, but then Cleveland is a very romantic city.

The romance of Cleveland runs deep and complicated, and part of the romance is tragic. We are guilty, you know. Corporate capitalism was born here at Standard Oil. We supplied the wars and the automobiles and polluted the river. We profited. We shut down the streetcars and built the suburbs. We lost the jobs. And we've done the time. We've suffered. We know the dark side of America. We've lived it and breathed it and we've fought it. That foreign bank that the US bailed out to the tune of $290 billion to prop up the global financial system, that pays its bankers more than Goldman Sachs? It owns those houses in our neighborhood that our community development organization keeps boarding back up. We live with the ruins of corporate capitalism.

When I worked for the Cleveland Urban Design Collaborative (CUDC), at one point we took on the task of designing a master plan for the Broadway Scenic Byway, which connects to the Ohio and Erie Canal Corridor. It turns out that just behind the main Cleveland Post Office the Byway ran past the original site of Standard Oil's first refinery, where Rockefeller forged new ground in horizontal and vertical integration, monopoly, economies of scale, abuse of natural resources, multinational investment, and contempt for labor, and became the richest man in the world. Rockefeller later left Cleveland for New York, harassed by Cleveland tax officials for the remainder of his life. The Standard Oil site was partly abandoned, with some container storage and a small plaque in front of a brick building commemorating the historic spot. We drew up a master plan envisioning an expansive overlook with interpretive signage and kiosks.

I can be dispassionately fascinated by the beauty of abandonment and loss in a photo of a vacant lot, an abandoned bridge, or a decaying warehouse and ignore the real ugly consequences of that loss. I'd call that looking at ruin porn. But if I acknowledge that we need to fight against the ugliness, that is part of the story, if the place is real to me, I don't call it ruin porn. If somebody's climbed up on that building to write "Read more books" at the top, if I know what was there before and hoped for what it could be, if I've stood by the fence and looked through it, if I've scrambled over the pile of bricks and taken a few home for my garden, if I respect it, if I care, I call it beautiful. I might call it romantic.

Not long after we completed our design for the Standard Oil interpretive site the existing plaque was stolen for scrap metal. Shortly thereafter a bridge on the road leading to the site was condemned and the main byway route closed. The site remains uncelebrated. It's about ten years later. There are some wildflowers. There are some gravel piles hidden by fencing overgrown with trees and vines. It's quiet. You probably wouldn't call it picturesque.

The birthplace of Standard Oil is there to find if you seek it out, and there's a stunning view of the steelyards on the way. It's a great place to think about things that once were, and contemplate the endless struggles of people and ideas that we are a part of today, and the romance of history.

You can have your Rust Belt Chic. I have my Rust Belt romance.

Pray for Cleveland: Reflections of an Investigative Reporter

Roldo Bartimole

I *came to Cleveland in the spring of 1965.* Walked out of Terminal Tower and headed up Euclid Avenue. I was eager for a reporting job in a major urban city. I walked to a job interview at the *Plain Dealer*.

Cleveland was a big city. More than 750,000. I could feel it pulsating as I walked. Tall buildings. Lots of people on the street. I came from Bridgeport, Conn., a city I've described as a small Cleveland. It had the same industrial, working-class character.

Now I've been a Clevelander for 47 years. It is my home. I see its warts and problems. Yet I find it satisfying. So what has Cleveland meant to me?

I quickly learned some about the culture of Cleveland in my first days here. In the *Plain Dealer* city room I encountered two characteristics that alerted me to problems. First, a tug-of-war among colleagues about where my family and I should live. West Side? East Side? Why should this be important? Clevelanders of the 1960s know the answer. West was white. East was black. I settled in Cleveland Heights, where I still reside. That conversation should have told me all I needed about the sharp racial divisions here.

The other question also surprised me. "What nationality are you?" they asked. That told me of another great division, of ethnicity. This was a city fragmented by ethnic and racial separations. It reflected in its politics and culture. Often heartbreakingly.

I've never been jingoistic about the city. My feeling is I could be living in any large city. I'd be doing the same as I am. You should not fall in love with a city or a nation. It's not healthy to view a city as a fan. Cities are not sports teams. They don't deserve boundless patriotism. You then tend to ignore its defects. This makes a region susceptible to charlatans.

I've been fortunate as a journalist to have reported at a time of urban upheaval and unrest. I learned much in a brief time. The times were explosive and revealing. Roiling waters divulge what calm waters hide. In crisis, major actors were required to leave backstage positions. They came into the open to be observed. What I saw made me a bitter foe of how things were done around here. I left the *PD* to start a small newsletter. I wrote as I wanted, about what I wanted. It lasted 32 years. Below is a recollection of some of the times I reported.

We have to remember Cleveland's history. It was born great: "At Cleveland iron ore met coal to become steel and rode off by railroad to build America's skyscrapers, railroads and bridge," a geography scholar once wrote. Cleveland's leaders adopted a similar grandiose air. It would impact Cleveland's evolution and devolution.

The city's oligarchic leaders were a tight-knit group. "We all belong to the Union Club. We all call each other. We have no hesitation to call each other for help," said one corporate leader in the 1960s. Its motto was reflected in the saying, "You may beat our Browns but you can't beat our Union Club."

Cleveland is a poverty-ridden city of great wealth. A lot of the wealth is old and parked in foundations. Foundations exert disproportionate power with an undeserved say in public decisions. Their wishes reflect the desires of wealth and board composition.

One example proves relevant. During the tough times of the 1960s, some church people wanted to bring the renowned organizer Saul Alinsky to Cleveland. The hope was his skills would help African Americans make gains. As a *Plain Dealer* reporter on this story, I called two of that period's top corporate leaders for their opinions. Ralph Besse, chairman of the board of the Cleveland Electric Illuminating Company (CEI) and head of the Inner City Action Committee, formed after the Hough riots, declared that the ghetto "doesn't need an agitator." Jack Reavis, managing partner of the city's largest law firm and leader of the

Businessmen's Interracial Committee, said a visit by Alinsky would be "a tragedy."

Both civic groups were foundation-funded. Both committees were formed because of the urgency of problems. These problems were revealed in Reavis' statement to the visiting US Civil Rights Commission in 1966: "It was the violence that really caused us to try to establish lines of communication . . . . Tempers and tensions were very high, indeed. I thought it quite possible that Cleveland would be the first of the Northern cities where savage violence might break out. . . ."

Eventually, Alinsky, came to Cleveland at the invitation of the Council of Churches. Black ministers denounced him and African American groups favored by corporate interests picketed his visit. Alinsky pulled no punches about his feelings of the local situation. He knew the dynamics here. He slammed Cleveland's African American leadership, saying, "Cleveland has a reputation of having a beaten Negro population." He went on: "Its leadership is pretty well bought out. That's your reputation."

There was another lesson to be learned. Besse, as head of CEI, had reason to want Mayor Ralph Locher out of office. CEI, a private utility, had been trying for decades to relieve Cleveland of its electric light system. The publicly owned Muni Light, as it was called, was not only a competitor but ideologically repugnant to the private corporation. Besse saw an opening.

He strategically had his Inner City Action Committee break with Mayor Locher. He personally rebuked the mayor in a bitter letter given to an excited media. The *PD* played the story with large, bold Page One headlines.

Besse made another move he kept secret. During all this unrest, Carl B. Stokes, an African American state legislator, vied with Mayor Locher in the Democratic primary of 1967. A riot would damage Stokes's chances. So Besse and other business people funded a secret program called "Peace in Cleveland." Payments went to black nationalists to keep racial peace. The crucial element, I found, was that the payments ended the weekend of the Democratic primary. It appeared Besse wanted racial peace that summer so Stokes would defeat pro-Muni Light Locher in the primary. Business leaders likely felt that Stokes could not win a head-to-head election with a white Republican candidate. The surprise was that Stokes won by a slim margin and became the first African

American mayor of a major US city.

The business leaders quickly moved to accept Stokes, running a full-page ad in the *Wall Street Journal* boasting of an old-line blue chip city with bright new leadership. They joined with Stokes in supporting a supposed anti-poverty drive called Cleveland Now! This came after Stokes and other black people walked the streets of Cleveland after the assassination of Martin Luther King, Jr. Cleveland was one of the major troubled cities that did not have riots after King's death.

But the marriage didn't last long. In 1968, using a program similar to Besse's, some of the same nationalists bought weapons with Cleveland Now! money. The guns were used in a shootout with police in Glenville. This soured relations between Stokes and corporate leaders.

This short description of this period in Cleveland hardly does justice to the severe strains it caused the city. Though the incendiary period of riot and disorder subsided, those troubles still remain in the public consciousness of the city. It was marked by car bumper stickers saying, "Pray for Cleveland."

Cleveland struggled through the 1970s with financial problems, a failed recall of Mayor Dennis Kucinich and a default. A T-shirt of the times told it all: "Cleveland—You Gotta Be Tough." In the 1980s, a different urban experience developed. The two-year dramatic reign of Mayor Kucinich brought the corporate community into the open again. Its leaders coalesced to oust Kucinich and move City Hall in a different direction.

Fortune Magazine had the best description of the corporate movement late in the 1980s. It described corporate actions here in military terms. *Fortune* claimed a corporate "cabal" overthrew Kucinich. The article was entitled, "How Business Bosses Saved a Sick City." It said:

E. Mandel de Windt, the now retired CEO of Eaton Corp. and unofficial dean of Cleveland businessmen, organized the troops and devised the strategy, setting in motion a benign conspiracy of executives and entrepreneurs that still operates. The impressive feat of organizing that cabal and persuading Cleveland's most senior businessmen to take charge of the grittiest aspects of civic life was the real key to the town's turnaround.

In other words, private interests took over the public agenda. That provided an important urban lesson in how the civic agenda becomes distorted by the major forces in a community. It also was a perfect civic barometer of "Who Rules?" The 1980s saw a concerted use of public power for private benefit. Particularly in how Cleveland's downtown developed.

The establishment really started in the 1970s by purchasing land where the Gateway sports facilities would eventually be built. Republican County Commissioner Vince Campanella proposed a property tax to fund a stadium. Voters knocked it out by a two-to-one count. It was only prelude to the 1990 push for a new $180 million stadium and $154 million arena, driven by Mayor Michael White and an aggressive corporate campaign to pass a "sin" tax, levied on liquor, wine, beer, and cigarettes. But Gateway costs zoomed. Cuyahoga County Commissioners issued bonds for $45 million and $75 million for overruns without a public vote. The citizens pay bondholders $8 to $10 million annually and will into 2023.

Other publicly subsidized ventures took root. The most opportunistic developer was Dick Jacobs. Jacobs made a good friend at City Hall with Council President George Forbes. Forbes and then-Mayor George Voinovich found ways to load Jacobs's pockets, all in the name of resurrecting Cleveland.

Jacobs—beyond receiving generous public subsidy for the Galleria downtown and the aforementioned Gateway project—really scored with a $10 million, zero-interest, 20-year loan for what is now the Key Center on the north side of Public Square. To spice things up, Forbes, with Mayor Voinovich, added tax abatement at 100 percent for 20 years! That alone was worth $120 million in relieved property taxes. With a zero interest loan, City Hall sweetened it by requiring no payment of principal until the end of 20 years. More was dished. Attached to the Key building was a Marriott Hotel, also built by Jacobs. He got another zero interest $10 million and 100 percent property tax abatement for 20 years on the hotel.

Free money was flowing out of City Hall. It was binge time.

Similarly, Forest City Enterprises lined up at the goodies table. At Tower City on Public Square, Forest City enjoyed the bounty of the times. The Avenue, a retail development in Tower City, was awarded a $10 million public subsidy. Other parts of the redevelopment of Terminal Tower received subsidies of $2.7 million and $2 million and $9.2 million for the adjacent old post office building. Public money poured into Public Square.

When Jacobs received hotel subsidies, Forest City, owners of the Ritz-Carlton hotel, were jealous. Demands were made. It received a $7.9 million subsidy and a 20-year, 100-percent tax abatement worth $34.5 million for its hotel.

Most of this public revenue lost hurt the Cleveland schools. Typically, the schools were to receive 50 percent or more of the county property tax revenue.

The *coup de grace* came at the end of the Forbes-Voinovich era in 1989, though the true nature of this power play wasn't revealed until the 1990s, when Mayor White sued Dick Jacobs. The legal discovery process revealed that Forbes and Voinovich—both with financially interested parties involved—negotiated a secret deal beneficial to their friends and associates. Forbes did business with Jacobs, and Voinovich's former law firm partner represented and was a board member of Figgie Corporation.

This venture, a proposed 530-acre development, was termed the "Figgie Project" after Harry Figgie, Chairman of the Figgie Corporation. It involved strategically located land owned by the city of Cleveland since Mayor Tom Johnson's time at the turn of the 20th century, though it was located outside the city limits. The deal was struck as both Council President Forbes and Mayor Voinovich were leaving City Hall. City Council had little input and details of the deal remained secret for years.

Legal discovery during the city's lawsuit revealed that Forbes secretly had inserted Jacobs into a dominant management position. Figgie departed and the project became known as Chagrin Highlands, a site described by a consultant as "without doubt one of the finest pieces of real estate between New York City and Chicago." It became a Jacobs-run venture.

Recently, Eaton Corporation uprooted itself from downtown Cleveland to move to its new $170 million headquarters in Chagrin Highlands. It was predictable that the site, aided by more than $100 million in Ohio highway funds for I-271 interchanges at its doorstep, would be a stiff competitor to downtown Cleveland.

Of course the situation is typical of Cleveland eating its own. That hasn't demonstrably changed to this day. Nor has the desperation in so many parts of Cleveland, and its continued drop in population.

The city I came to has shrunk below 400,000. But those who rebelled in the '60s are quiet, or violence is no longer visible or threatening to the larger community. So the power people simply leave them alone to whatever fate awaits them.

Strange Love, or how we stopped bitching and learned to love Cleveland

Kevin Hoffman and Thomas Francis

Y*ou will never see a movie* where a cat like Humphrey Bogart looks at a dame like Ingrid Bergman and says, "We'll always have Cleveland." Except if it's a comedy.

Halle Berry was born in Cleveland. She's not coming back.

While watching MTV, you will never hear the words "*Real World Cleveland.*"

Johnny Depp does not own a bar here.

In Chicago, Eliot Ness was "untouchable." In Cleveland, he was "safety director."

Our beaches aren't golden. Our industry isn't high-tech. Our sports teams can't win. And every once in a while, we fuck something up and the whole Northeast goes black.

Guess what? None of this bothers us. Because we've been talking with our fellow Clevelanders, and there's no shame in their game. They're not trapped here like lost dogs in an animal shelter. They're here because they want to be, because they know what we know: that Cleveland is the pinnacle of modern civilization, the closest mankind has come to achieving an ideal society. And this near-utopia shines with particular brilliance for that demographic over which every city drools: the young professional. That's right. If you're college-educated, ambitious, worldly, and between the ages of 20 and 40, you've reached Shangri-La. All that you want is here.

You Can Get Your Rocks Off

As Paul McCartney's solo career proved, bad music happens when a rocker becomes happy and well-adjusted. Fortunately, there are legions of jaded, disaffected young Clevelanders, and out of this milieu, a gritty, badass brand of rock is born.

Cleveland rock doesn't have a unified sound. The bands connect on a deeper level. "It's more of a cynical, hard-ass, devil-may-care attitude—and that comes out lyrically," says Frank Mauceri, founder of Smog Veil, a punk label in Reno, Nevada. "I've traveled all around, and I just don't see that attitude in L.A. or Austin or New York City."

The Rock Hall is for tourists. Real rock lovers make pilgrimages to the Beachland, the Agora, and the Grog Shop.

All the bands that hit Seattle, San Francisco, and Austin also play Cleveland. We're centrally located. They can't avoid us. The difference is that here you get to see them on the cheap, at more intimate venues. And after the show, they might ask to crash on your couch.

We've Got Your Culture Right Here, Pal!

We've heard people complain that there's no "culture" here. By that, we think they mean something more than a ribfest headlined by a Duran Duran cover band.

Want some culture? Take down these directions: Go north of I-480, take a left at your earlobe, and look right under your goddamn nose. Everything your cultural heart desires is in metropolitan Cleveland.

Cleveland ain't Manhattan, but when it comes to plays, it's the next best thing. As performing arts districts go, only Broadway is bigger than Playhouse Square. We get our share of art-house flicks as well.

So we're not lacking for arts and entertainment. We're just lacking a little appreciation for what we've got.

"The negative views come from people who don't actually utilize what we have," says Dave Sharkey, communications director for Progressive Urban Real Estate. "Have you gone to the art museum lately? To a show at Playhouse Square? To the Warehouse District to check out the action? My guess is, there's a lot of people that just don't realize that this exists here, but then they'll go to Chicago and say, 'This is great.'"

Which means that if you're sitting at home bored, it might be because you're boring.

Livin' Large on Low Wages

Our generation has sailed into the economic equivalent of *The Perfect Storm*: a housing crisis, a jobless recovery, and a prolonged recession. So it's best to seek shelter in a city where you can still pretend to be a pimp even if you're scraping by as a bike messenger. That would be Lakewood.

Let's say you're making $27,000 in Cleveland—struggling but surviving. Just to live the same lifestyle in Chicago, you'd have to be making $35,000. In New York, you'd need $47,000. In San Francisco, you'd have to more than double your salary.

Jennifer Bargiel learned that the hard way. A 29-year-old interior designer at Arhaus in the Flats, she grew up in Solon and moved to New York to be a model. She was making about the same money as in Cleveland, only in the Big Apple it wasn't enough to purchase either comfort or security.

"It was the tiniest frickin' thing you've ever seen," says Bargiel of her $800-a-month Staten Island apartment, "and it was me, my husband, and my dog. Two weeks after I moved there, my car got stolen. A month after that, my husband's bike got stolen!"

So Uncool, It's Cool

Look at Harvey Pekar. Okay, not directly at him. But consider his achievement: he proved that an ornery guy from Cleveland could get a major Hollywood film made about his life.

There's a little bit of Harvey in all of us. It's not that we're born losers. It's just that we don't give a rat's ass about image.

We know that our women don't all look like Mimi from *The Drew Carey Show*, that Drew's not the quintessential Cleveland Man, and that even lovable losers like Dennis Kucinich are mascots, not symbols.

Besides, any scholar will tell you that coolness follows a 180-degree arc. The very act of *trying* makes you a poseur, because it's self-conscious, which is the uncoolest thing on the planet.

In other cities, people are trying way too hard. You see it on Miami's South Beach, where even parking-lot attendants have $1,000-a-month coke habits. You see it on the Sunset Strip in L.A., where the fake tits outnumber college degrees. Even in Chicago—a Midwestern city, for chrissakes!

The Road Less Traveled

Heat steams up from the freeway. The AC is maxed out and you're still sweating through your pants. Two cups of coffee are screaming to escape your bladder. And some asshole is trying to cram his Beamer into your lane, which hasn't moved in nine minutes.

Welcome to the big city, kid.

It could be the I-405 in Los Angeles. It could be another summer clogged by construction on Chicago's I-94. All we know is, those who live in Cleveland remain blissfully naive to the ways of major-league gridlock.

"Out there, road rage is a daily event," says Tim Meacham, who spent 90 minutes on his morning commute to D.C. from his house in the 'burbs. Now he commutes from Hudson to downtown Cleveland. It's the same distance, but it takes only 35 minutes.

What good is it to be in a city with great cultural institutions, if it's too daunting to drive to them? Add up the hours you spend in traffic, and subtract that from your leisure time.

"My wife and I have done more cultural things in Cleveland than we did in D.C.—and I think it's because we have a little bit more time," says Meacham. In D.C., "it was just a pain in the butt to get downtown."

Okay, so I-77 and I-480 are no picnic. But complaining about those freeways to people in other metropolises is like bitching about your toothache to a guy with the Ebola virus.

Where Vice Is Your Right

We all have vices. And when it comes to the classics—booze, nicotine, and fatty foods—Cleveland knows no peer.

Every city has dive bars. But Cleveland wins with volume. *Men's Fitness* says we have the third most per capita—as if we should be ashamed of that. Alcohol helps shy people make friends and ugly people get laid. It's doing God's work.

And we're not going to feel guilty about our collective paunch. It's easier to stay thin if you live in a warm climate (California) or if you have no choice but to walk everywhere (New York).

They starve. We feast. Cleveland wins again.

Stay and Make It Big

Prevailing wisdom says you have to leave for New York or L.A. to realize your dreams. The people following this wisdom are usually suckers. Thanks in large part to this myth, such cities will always have a generous supply of hookers.

Many of us have learned that we can become a smash without slashing our roots. There's no better example than Iron Chef Michael Symon, who cooked at fine restaurants in New York and Chicago, only to come back to Cleveland to launch Lola, the bistro of his dreams.

"When I started getting a lot of national exposure, a lot of my regular customers worried that I was going to leave Cleveland," says Symon. "I told them, if I was able to get that exposure in my hometown, there's no reason I should ever leave now. The only reason I would have ever thought of leaving is if I thought that being in Cleveland stunted my growth as a chef. And it hasn't."

In other cities, a restaurant with subpar food might be able to get by on celebrity credentials, manufacturing an air of exclusivity, or anything else that distracts from the product. That doesn't work in Cleveland.

So here's the point: If you're here, you're Cleveland. And if you really think about it, you're damn lucky.

—A version of this piece appeared in *Cleveland Scene*

IV. Growing Up

Bob Perkowski

When the Number 9 Bus Was Like Home, and Downtown Was My Playground

Sean Decatur

I *strained my neck to look* down the row of occupied orange seats to see who was getting on the bus. A big crowd—I should slide over close to the window, scrunching my book bag on my lap, leaning my head against the window, closing my eyes, pretending to sleep, one eye partially open to see who would sit next to me. The bus was already full, and we were only at East 55th Street. The bus was full of strangers who were also friendly and familiar: some faces I'd see each day, some that I would greet, some that would start up a casual conversation.

Five days a week, for about six years, the Number 9 bus was a morning and afternoon home away from home, a place where I could finish homework, take a nap, or eat a snack (if I remembered to bring one). I boarded at 12th and Euclid, right in front of the old Halle's building, just a block away from my apartment building (the then relatively new Park Centre complex at 12th and Chester—the European spelling of "Centre" always felt a bit out of place in the otherwise down-to-earth downtown neighborhood). I'd ride past Cleveland State (then primarily the Rhodes and Fenn towers); past the long stretch of old houses, former mansions, some boarded up, all showing their age; through the lively intersection at E. 105th and Euclid, where the "community billboard" posted by Winston Willis gave regular updates on his struggles to hold onto the land (and warned, prophetically, of the coming Clinic empire); through University Circle and though Little Italy, in the days before cafés

105

lined the sidewalks; past the Lakeview Cemetery (with its imposing gates and tall stone monuments visible from the road); by Coventry, eventually the hangout place of choice for my wannabe-hipster friends; beyond Severance Center, when it was a real mall (not a Walmart), with a two-screen movie theater and a Hough Bakery; through the manicured suburbia of Cleveland Heights; and eventually to the edge of the posh Gates Mills suburbs at the sleepy Eastgate Mall and then the private high school where I was a student.

The bus ran slowly in the winter when passengers had to leap over the large slush puddles at the curb to board; it was hot in September and May. I got to see the buses change over time—the older buses, without air conditioning and with old-fashioned cords to pull when your stop was coming up. These were replaced by MARTA buses, hand-me-downs to Cleveland from the Atlanta transit system, the faded outlined of the "MA" still visible despite the attempt to convert MARTA to RTA. Then came the new buses, with bright orange seats with brown plastic backs (did RTA adopt those colors because of the Browns?) and windows that didn't open but with air-conditioning on board. I saw those buses become worn too, windows forced open when the air-conditioning didn't work, vinyl seats slashed open, graffiti on the seat backs.

This trip through the city on generations of buses took me through the Cleveland that some would call gritty, a place some suburbanites kept at arm's length. But to me, equipped with a teen's ability to find creative outlets in any environment, downtown Cleveland was a wonderful playground: My geeky friends and I would go to retro films at CSU (I vividly remember a *M.A.S.H./Catch-22* double-feature—a dream for geeky, literary teen boys of the 1980s); I had Chester Commons (now Perk Park), with its Day-Glo striped paint on giant concrete walls as my own private skateboard park, and during the summer, I would delight in going to a different place—the old Erieview Fountains, the Malls, Chester Commons—for a different food truck lunch experience long before food trucks were cool (the best steakburgers I've ever had were grilled on a truck in Cleveland in the 1980s). I spent many Saturday afternoons in the awesome video arcade in the Colonial Arcade.

I was delighted when I had the chance to bring my suburban friends into downtown, or when school field trips would bring all of us to the theaters downtown—on the reverse of my commute. What was a daily ritual for me was an exotic voyage for those who only rarely descended from the Heights. I still remember the controversy when my school chose to have its prom at the Old Arcade (perhaps an early sign of newly emerging "Rust Belt Chic" aesthetic, but more likely part of the preppy phenomenon of the 1980s known as "slumming"); some parents insisted that the voyage into downtown (at night!) was too dangerous for their children, so a school bus shuttled the students from the 'burbs to the appealing but fearsome downtown in sheltered safety.

I left Cleveland long ago, only to return recently to Northeast Ohio. I am bemused to find that the concept of "Rust Belt Chic" is all the buzz, that the environment that I took for granted is now the rage, the cool place to live and play. The fantasy of my early teen years was that I would one day be a member of the hipster set. Perhaps unbeknownst to me or my friends, I was cool all along, and now the rest of the world has caught up.

Yet it was neither "grit" nor "chic" that made Cleveland (and my bus voyages) feel like home, that make these memories so vivid: It was the friendliness, the vibrant atmosphere, and the sense of community on those crowded buses.

When I come into downtown Cleveland today, I still marvel at the new things (the crowds on East 4th, folks rushing to the theater in Playhouse Square, a baseball stadium that actually has unobstructed views of the field); take in reminders of the past (the buildings that I will always refer to as "Higbee's," "May Company," and "Halle's," or my old apartment building, which is now an Embassy Suites hotel); and annoy my children by regularly pointing out the things, now long gone, that I still remember (the old Ninth Street Pier, the storefronts that used to be comic book shops or video arcades). To some, it is old and gritty; to some chic and hip; for me, more simply, it's home.

Letting Go of the Stats

Noreen Malone

N*ot so long ago,* the man I was seeing asked to borrow a book. He scanned my shelves, full of Alice Munro and Edith Wharton and the Marys (Karr, Gaitskill, McCarthy) and exactly all the sort of things you'd reliably expect a 27-year-old Brooklyn journalist of the white-wine-or-whiskey drinking variety to keep on hand, until he hit on something unexpected: *The Summer Game,* a Roger Angell ode to base-ball that I'd grabbed from my childhood bedroom the last time I was home. He began flipping through, wondering if I'd actually read it, and out fell my bookmark from when I had: a 1999 ticket to Section 555 of Jacobs Field, where my family had split season tickets, all through the good years for the Tribe—and the awkward years for me

This is the fifth baseball season I've been in New York, and my ninth away from Cleveland. This is the ninth season where I haven't known the Indians' utility players' biographies. The eighth, maybe, where I haven't known the left-handed setup guy's name. The seventh where I haven't known who was on the chopping block at the trade deadline. The sixth where I haven't known anyone's batting average. The fifth where I haven't known the starting lineup. The fourth that I have actively tried and carelessly failed to become a Mets fan. The third where I stopped noticing that I didn't really know who was the Tribe's closer. The second where I have felt, occasionally, like one of those terrible girls who fakes being into sports because she thinks it seems situationally appealing. The first where I have worried that this is a permanent condition.

It wouldn't matter so much if I hadn't been so convinced, once upon a time, that I was a baseball purist. And I really *was*. I was. I didn't just read the Angell, I read about anything I could get my hands on that would explain how, exactly, a knuckleballer gripped the ball, and why, exactly, one might possibly have given the bunt sign with two outs when it seemed so boneheaded. I listened to all of AM 1220 instead of the Backstreet Boys. I absorbed all I could from the Mikes (Hargrove, Trivisanno, Hegan). I picked number 13 for my softball jersey in tribute to Omar Vizquel, exactly the kind of consistent, singles-hitting, hardworking, charming, defensively brilliant player I thought represented the best of baseball. I had philosophies about the best of baseball, you see, and despite my shyness I'd launch into them with anyone who indicated even in the slightest that they might be willing to entertain them. I knew who the Indians needed to trade for. I read the sports section first, and often last, and always exhaustively.

It wasn't that I was a tomboy, exactly, though that was part of it. I was smart and bookish and chubby but athletic, and so baseball felt tailor-made for me, in all of those things. That I was a girl just made me feel a little more special about it. That the Indians were good, just when I needed baseball to be there, was probably one of the great strokes of luck I've had so far. They seemed then as permanent a part of me as my red hair or five siblings or that one freckle on my right ankle that I remember staring at on my first, nervous day of kindergarten, and my first, nervous day of college.

And here I am, writing at the All-Star break—at least I assume it's almost the All-Star break—and I don't know where the Indians are in the standings. It's really not that I've changed so much, although I suppose I don't stare at my ankles very much any more. In most things, I have never felt so much myself, as if the externalities have melted away to leave only what I need and want. And it seems I don't need baseball, even if I want to need it. If I did, I would have really worked at Mets fandom. (It really does require work—that's one of the familiar bits for a Clevelander used to post- or mid-season disappointment.) Or I'd have given in to the dark allure of the Yankees. (No. No!!) Or maybe just paid attention to the Indians via the wonders of the Internet, which is embarrassingly, devastatingly easy for someone with a desk job.

What I've figured out, though, is that maybe I didn't want base-ball—I wanted Cleveland. I wanted to walk from the stadium past Tower City to my dad's office parking lot at 11:34 pm after a Tribe game on a hot August night, knowing I'd be tired for morning swim practice but caught up in the swirling, ecstatic crowd walking outside the Gund, of guys in black sneakers and ladies with bra straps exposed and tans darker than the Cuyahoga in December, who'd had a few too many Bud Lights, and who seemed, to my protected Shaker Heights eye, like creatures from another planet that I wanted to visit but was scared to zoom into.

I wanted to get in my dad's green Buick and hear those same people call in to the post-game show, to vent, in slightly soused tones, about how rotten the seventh-inning pitching switch had been. I wanted to hear the host cut them off and go to commercial break because it was the only way out. I wanted to pull up to a traffic light at North Park and Lee and hear my dad chuckle about how Charlie Manuel never said anything, not really, and yet he couldn't help being charmed. I wanted to be able to impress my brothers with my knowledge of the Indians' road record, and to have something to talk about with the husbands who awkwardly drove me home from babysitting jobs and the cousins I saw twice a year and the boys I had crushes on. I wanted to know that I was rooting for the same thing as my dying grandmother and parish priest and unborn nephews and nieces and maybe one day daughters and sons of my own.

I still want these things, maybe; I wanted a community with per-manence, even though I forget it too often. I don't have any of it now, though I have plenty of other things I thought I wanted.

I guess no one knows how things will end up when you're just at the All-Star break, though.

The Lake Effect

David Giffels

T*he winter of my 16th year,* my dad got tickets to a football playoff game in Cleveland, the Browns against the Oakland Raiders, and he and my two brothers and I rode up in one of his engineering firm's beat-up surveying vans, all of us bundled against the cold. My dad always bought vehicles with a profound antithesis of style: three-on-the-tree, pie-pan hubcapped, olive drab tin boxes with a blank plate where the AM radio belonged. Hard vinyl bench seats. No carpet. No ceiling padding. Even with the heat on full blast, the inside of the van felt like a meat locker. The interior was caked with dried mud and smelled strongly of last summer's mosquito repellent, cut with the sweet lumbery pine of the wooden property stakes that clattered around in the rear. My older brother Ralph had tied his orange plastic kid-size Browns helmet to the top of the van with clothesline. Slapped together on the cheap, we looked like everyone else driving into Cleveland that day.

There was never any color in the 30 miles of sky between Akron and Cleveland. It was a masterpiece of monochrome. Until you hit the city limits. There, the celestial flatness was spiked by a huge steel-factory smokestack with giant fantastical flames roaring out its top. It looked exactly like hell and smelled worse. That's how we knew we were in Cleveland.

The temperature that day was four degrees; the wind-chill was 36 below. At the time, it was the second-coldest NFL playoff game ever

111

played, which is uncannily correct. When you live in a place like this, you come to understand that we are never first. In anything. Not even misery. The second most-frigid game in history?

Yes. Exactly.

We parked as close as we could get to the stadium, which stood like some outpost of the Great Depression at the edge of Lake Erie's polluted gunmetal waters. My dad had a spare pair of galoshes in the back of the truck, surveyor's boots. Before we locked up and started our walk to the stadium, he told me to put them on, but I refused. They didn't look cool. I was wearing my black high-top Chuck Taylors, and there was no way I'd be seen in front of 80,000 people sporting those hideous boots.

I'd never been to a Browns game before. I had no idea that the entire crowd would be dressed like some hybrid of a Dickens backstreet throng and a post-apocalyptic hunting party. Here, camouflage was the mark of a Sunday dandy. These fans, three abreast on the sidewalk toward Cleveland Municipal Stadium, were a cattle call of dull parkas topped with bulbous, oversize jerseys; fatsos in earflaps; drunks with double-layered blankets wrapped crooked around their torsos. Meaty men layered in flannel with two-week beards and stretched-out stocking caps. Women in mismatched gloves and padded hunting pants. They looked like a rogue regiment of Michelin Men. We joined them in the long slow walk up East Ninth Street toward the colorless hulking stadium, its countless tons of dumped concrete tracked with wooden seats.

I, still clinging to the potential street credibility of my footwear, was a decided outsider. I was casually interested in the Browns, in football, in sports. But as family dynamics go, I was a rank amateur. While I was reading Sherlock Holmes stories, my brother Ralph was memorizing the Browns media guide. His favorite pastime was being quizzed on arcane roster details:

Brian Sipe?

Quarterback! Number 17! San Diego State!

Major?

Architecture!

Dave Logan?

Receiver! Number 85! Colorado State!

Hometown?

Fargo! North Dakota!

And so on.

It wasn't until we approached the stadium gates that I began to feel something of the upsweep. And then there it was, as sudden and profound as the olfactive poignancy of a hog pen: the spirit of thousands, roughing out their ardor. The city smelled of barrel fires and roasted hot dogs and cold wool: the aluminum tang of a Cleveland January. But the sound is what defined the day—spontaneous group cheers delivered in bellowing choruses:

Here we go Brownies, here we go! Whoo! Whoo!

We made our way through the gate and entered the immense, creaky old concourse, pigeons roosting in the rafters above, paint cracked and peeling from the supports, piss trickling from the restroom troughs. The sound here intensified, like a freight train in a tunnel.

Let's go Browns!

Let's go Browns!

Let's go Browns!

They cared, but even with something as overt as football, it wasn't entirely clear what they cared about. It seemed to be more than just the outcome of the game. We climbed the cement stairs to the bleachers, entering a vast roaring stadium, ungodly cold. There was a rancid spice of hot chocolate and cigar smoke. From our seats behind the goalpost, I could see mounds of snow plowed along the sidelines, where the players, all with long sleeves under their jerseys, danced in place, blowing thick steam into their hands, waiting for the game to start. They seemed to move in slow motion. The playing surface looked different than it did on television, and my dad explained to me that it was mostly dirt, but the groundskeepers painted it green to look better on camera.

Three men behind us were passing a Thermos back and forth and when the game began and the Raiders quarterback, Jim Plunkett, took the field, one of them started hooting out, "Ya fuckin' Indian!"

The reference was loose at best. Plunkett's parents were Mexican-American. But that mattered little. As the game went on, "fuckin' Indian" rolled from the trio of Thermos-drinkers behind us nearly as often of the deafening, hair-raising roar of *DEE-FENSE* overtook the stadium. If I was looking for a sound to define my day, that chant was the answer. It would begin small, somewhere indistinct, like a random match dropped in a dry forest, a single voice: *Dee-fense.* A section of the stadium would call back in response: *DEE-fense!* Then half the stadium, and by the fourth or fifth round, the syllables would thunder—*DEE! FENSE!*—from deep in the guts of every one of the 80,000 of us, a bellow of shared passion for stopping someone who was trying to push us around.

We could do it with our voices. We could stop the Raiders. We were vital. All we had to do was make ourselves known, to roar back into the mouth of Lake Erie.

The cold was brutal. I couldn't understand how the players were able to catch a hard football or run into one another. Everything I touched felt like it would shatter. My eyeballs were made of candy glass. My lips were hardened Silly Putty. Packed tight between my brothers, I kept dropping to my seat to rub my hands together between my knees. By the end of the first quarter, I couldn't feel my toes and was nearly in tears as I bounced on the soles of my thin woeful sneakers, desperate for warmth.

"I told you you should have put on those boots," my dad said.

I refused to admit my pride.

Down on the field, the players seemed to be playing against the weather even more than themselves. Brian Sipe, the Browns quarterback, the SoCal native, looked desperate, with a turtleneck underneath his jersey, hands crammed into pockets sewn to the front. He looked as cold as I felt. When he dropped back to pass and tried to set his feet, he would slide on the icy brown-green surface. Offense was nearly nonexistent. Running plays looked like the ones my brother and I concocted on the vibrating metal sheet of our Coleco electric football game, stiff-armed footballers pushing chaotically against one another without advancing. The two teams traded punts and interceptions, neither ever really moving the ball.

Halfway through the second quarter, I couldn't take the cold anymore and my dad sent me down to walk around in the concourse, where he thought it might be a little warmer. He didn't want me to go alone, but there was no way he was missing this. So my 11-year-old brother Louis and I tramped down the stairs to the filthy promenade. It smelled like beer and piss and the flaccid perfume of boiled frankfurters. As we made our way through the interior, the sound of the slightly distant crowd was almost haunting:

DEE-FENSE ... DEE-FENSE ... DEE-FENSE ...

But then, all at once, it changed. The sound rose above its already impossible volume, a cacophonous roar. Something was happening ... something big ... something from which we had been omitted.

Louis looked at me.

"Shit," he said, a word he'd just learned from the Thermos drinkers.

He knew I'd made him miss something, and even then his freckled baby face seemed to reveal a bitter wisdom, that this was something he would regret in something like a historic way. We raced back to our section, catching the scoreboard on the way.

Browns: 6

Raiders: 0

"You missed it!" Ralph screamed, wild-eyed, holding his hands against the sides of his stocking cap. "Bolden intercepted! He ran it back for a touchdown!"

The three men behind us were a tangle of arms and blankets and slaps and head-bumps.

"Take that, ya fuckin' Indian!"

The Browns lined up to kick the extra point. As Don Cockroft gingerly made his approach on the frozen mud, a Raiders player blasted through the line and blocked the kick.

The game continued on this way, a constant struggle for footing, for position, for inches of advantage. Failure. Failure. Failure. All afternoon, the wind kept ripping in from Lake Erie. The old concrete of Cleveland Municipal Stadium felt like glacial ice and it just hurt, all of it: the cold, the frustration, the brutal brotherhood of violence.

By the fourth quarter, the Thermos drinkers had fallen into bouts of slurred, profane nonsense, blasting racist spittle toward Plunkett. The game had continued in a series of jabs and punts and miscues. Sipe threw an interception. Reggie Rucker dropped a touchdown pass in the end zone. Cockroft missed a field goal. Plunkett was sacked and fumbled. Cockroft missed another. The Raiders crashed clumsily into the end zone.

The Browns were down 14-12 with less than a minute to go. Finally finding a frantic groove, they had driven the ball to the Raiders' 13-yard line. It was third down. Sipe called a timeout. Everyone in the stadium was standing, bobbing with anticipation. Eight thousand of us.

Although I was squeezed parka-to-parka among the men of my family, I didn't feel warm, but I did feel something oddly similar to warmth: a shared coldness. Most of the seats in that ungainly stadium were "obstructed view," and part of the nuance of viewing a game there was adjusting position to see around the rusty, paint-chipped posts and I-beams supporting the upper decks. We were all huddled close, the swish of nylon against nylon, the heavy murmur of anticipation, all of us sharing a calculation of the odds. All we needed was a field goal. No further than an extra point. Then hold the Raiders for the remaining few seconds and this will all have been worth it.

The offense came back out onto the field. They lined up tight. Sipe raised his arms wide as he approached the line, trying to quiet the crowd. He leaned over the center, received the snap, looked across the end zone, drew back his arm and released. The ball headed toward the goal line, toward the corner, toward tight end Ozzie Newsome, but it didn't look right, didn't zip through the air, was wobbling, caught up in the lake effect wind, just long enough for a stumbling white jersey to cut in front of Newsome, the ball absorbed into the Stickum-slathered arms of one of the Raiders, of someone who would be flying straight to California after this was done.

Intercepted.

The stadium fell silent. Browns players shrunk from the celebration. The Raiders ran out the remaining seconds. It was over. Three weeks later they would win the Super Bowl. Everyone around us, wrapped in blankets and ponchos, looked dazed. What happened? We would soon learn that during the timeout, head coach Sam Rutigliano had called for a pass to the corner of the end zone, a play called Red Right 88. If no one was open, he'd told Sipe, "throw it to the blonde in the second row." That would leave one more play for the chip-shot field goal. But Sipe had tried to force the throw and that was that. He tried because he believed, and that was the biggest mistake.

He should have known.

Not Bullet Points, or I Remember Cleveland

Susan Grimm

H*ow do you stake a claim*—the chips from my front teeth on Daisy Avenue, the shoes I almost lost in new I-90 mud. My dead planted like stone flowers in Riverside and Holy Cross. I have always lived in Cleveland, and Cleveland has always been mine, even when I wanted to move away. Lilacs, hydrangeas, bridal veil.

My parents came to the city in the first half of the 20th century. I like to imagine dotted lines stitching up the map from the river towns of Ohio and West Virginia or spiraling the hills and pastures of PA. One of my mother's brothers brought my father home for supper when they both worked at Republic Steel. My father was walking to Republic, then, from Macedonia. Later, he and his brother bought a second-hand car.

After World War II, when my mother and father married, they were supported by steel in their two-family house on Mapledale Avenue, the upstairs always rented to a family member (my mother having given up whichever job—printer's assistant, Ohio Bell operator, lunch counter girl—to stay home). Front porches, tree lawns, roller skating on sidewalks made of slate.

I can remember my grandmother and her daughters talking in Slovak. *Halupki, palacinki.* I can remember weddings at church auditoriums and VFW halls where everyone under 12 slid assiduously on the wood floor. Bus rides before air conditioning when the wind might whip in some pollutionary flecks. A ride on the Goodtime with money we'd earned from a doll-clothes sale. Piano lessons in a partitioned Euclid Avenue mansion next to the Al Koran Shrine Temple.

The howling of the zoo animals (anecdotal). Hearing Ferlinghetti read in the aisles of a church downtown. Schroeder's. Publix. The train station under the Terminal Tower when it still had trains. When downtown was the fat body of the spider drawing everyone in. RTA/CTS.

Potholes I have chucked. Trees I have climbed. Beers I have drunk. We crunched Sabin sugar cubes (polio) three blocks from home at Denison School. Graduating in the last class from Lourdes Academy. St. Michael's crowd of statues on Scranton Road. Blue nuns. Walking downtown over the Detroit-Superior Bridge. The Cleveland Public Library—Brooklyn Branch.

Higbee's. Halle's. The free bus that shuttled in between. Silver Grille. Minotaur Room. Bacon sandwiches at Taylor's Rolling Cart. When greenhouses rimmed the flats on Schaaf Road. When the Galleria had stores.

The first orchestra concert for the Fourth of July on Public Square. The Art Museum courtyard that's been designed away. Movies at the Palace, the Hippodrome. The early days of the Poets' League of Greater Cleveland and a winter party at Barbara Angell's house. Junkstock and other Daniel Thompson-orchestrated moments where poetry became event. Accordions. *Ghoulardi. The Gene Carroll Show.* The garden outside the old stadium when there was only one.

"There's Always Next Year"

Annie Zaleski

My *father was born in 1949.*

If you're a lifelong Indians fan, his birth year is significant. Chances are, you're shaking your head in sympathy or smiling ruefully right about now. My long-suffering father has never seen his beloved team win the World Series. He missed the chance to experience a world championship by less than a year.

I take comfort in the fact that he's at least seen the Indians in the World Series. In 1954—when the team was swept by the New York Giants—he and his dad watched a game on a tiny black-and-white television with fuzzy reception. In 1997, we bundled up in winter clothes to sit in the bleachers at Jacobs Field to watch the team face the Florida Marlins.

Of course, the Indians lost both of those series.

To this day, any mention of the 1997 postseason elicits grumbles and sighs from my father. Mention Jose Mesa, the relief pitcher who squandered the Indians' 2–1 lead—and, as it turned out, the championship—and this grumbling intensifies. But this ostensibly lighthearted grousing isn't exactly innocuous. The look on his face when talking about this near-miss—his eyes softened by sadness and inescapable flashbulb memories of the team's collapse—reveals the enduring impact of loss. It was the closest he had come in his lifetime to seeing the Indians win the World Series—and it was perhaps the best chance he'd ever have to see them win.

My stoic father would never admit this out loud, of course. But intuitively, I understand why he winces. I was there with him in our family room that night in 1997, hopping around excitedly as we watched the game, daring to dream of an Indians championship after so many years of futility. I still empathize with the emotional aftermath of this loss, a sucker punch to optimism which deflated us both. We fell just short of victory together.

Indeed, my dad and I always bonded over Cleveland sports—especially baseball. My mother and younger brother were indifferent (if not apathetic) to the Indians, but I became hooked after going to my first game in 1986, a wide-eyed first grader awed by the game's excitement. During the late '80s, when the upper deck of cavernous Cleveland Municipal Stadium was often nothing but empty sickly-yellow chairs, we went to games religiously. Watching the Indians lose was a shared ritual for us. My dad and I could always find common ground in a terrible baseball team, even if we butted heads on everything else.

Our special relationship to baseball mirrored the one my dad had with his mom, herself a rabid baseball fan until the day she died. (In her later years, Paul Sorrento and Brook Jacoby were two of her favorites, and she had cable strictly so she could watch the games.) In August 1959, she took him to see the Indians face the White Sox. The team was neck-and-neck with its Chicago rivals for first place, and 70,000 people had flocked to the stadium.

As my father recalls, the Indians lost that game (and the rest of the pivotal series, too). But that year—thanks in no small part to her gesture—he became a "live or die" fan of the team. He started collecting baseball cards, which survived his childhood in pristine shape because he was an only child. Listening to the Indians on the radio became a staple; seeing televised games—a much rarer occurrence back then—was a special treat. Much later, he and one of his best friends (my godfather, in fact) stood in long lines at Ten Cent Beer Night, before the game ended in forfeit because of a drunken riot. He saw Frank Robinson debut as the first African American manager in baseball, and went to Opening Day every year, like clockwork.

After he and my mom married, my dad connected with her relatives over his love of baseball. My great-grandparents would drag lawn chairs outside their apartment at the intersection of West 110th and Detroit. Radio between them, they would spend warm summer nights together, listening to the games. My great-grandfather used to talk Indians with my dad, because my dad "was the only one who cared."

Indeed, my dad has always had faith in the potential of the team. Each new season brings a clean slate—and the possibility that this year things would click for the Indians, even if last season produced, say, 100-plus losses. But this success could be just around the corner. We even bought a 20-game season ticket package in 1993, because it meant we had first dibs on tickets for the shiny new ballpark—as if a different locale meant a change in fortune.

Still, my dad comes to his optimism with wariness and pragmatism. Being an Indians fan is less about dramatic losses and more about sustained, prolonged mediocrity—the dull ache of average baseball. He acknowledges this, but doesn't let precedent ruin his love for the team. If anything, he relishes their underdog nature, the fact that the Indians are (generally) never expected to be competitive or successful. It's a humble way to approach sports fandom that's very much in line with his personality—and very much how he taught me to love the Indians.

Because my dad was used to ineffectual baseball, I too learned early to temper my expectations when it came to the Indians. Expect to be let down, and then be pleasantly surprised with success—although this was obviously temporary, so I should enjoy it while it lasts. Love the Indians unconditionally—but be aware of what you're getting yourself into.

Recently, I asked my dad what keeps him a fan—why he still spends most summers on the couch in the air conditioning, watching the Indians on TV. Without missing a beat, he responded, "Because I'm a born Clevelander. I live and die by Cleveland sports."

He chuckled as he said this, as if the answer was obvious. "As a Clevelander, you should know that by now," he added, to underscore the preposterous foundation of my question.

While other major league teams are perennial losers, being an Indians fan requires a very specific mindset, one unique to—and ingrained in—Clevelanders: Throw together hope, cynicism, frustration and nostalgia—and a ton of blind faith to balance it all out. Today's Indians might break your heart, but tomorrow's team just might make it soar. And even if they don't? Well, to paraphrase a famous baseball quote, there's always next year.

Rust Belt Dreams

Connie Schultz

E *arlier this summer,* I was talking to a stranger at an out-of-state reception when his wife walked up, bumped her hip against his and said, "I need some cash."

"Why?" he said as he reached for his wallet.

She pointed to the bartender at the far end of a big outdoor tent. "I want to give him a tip for my drink."

Her husband fanned a few bills. She plucked two singles and he shook his head. "You don't need to tip him. He's taken care of."

I cleared my throat. "Really, he's probably not," I said, and gave a short tutorial on what my years of reporting have unearthed about unfair practices in the service industry.

"Far too often," I said, "management skims the tips."

The wife smiled, but her husband frowned. "Well, even so," he said, "guys like that know that people don't tip at these kind of things. He's not expecting it."

So not the point, I thought. *So not like Cleveland.*

I'm not one to romanticize the Midwest, or the working class. Born and raised in both, I know we have our share of ne'er-do-wells, as my great-grandmother used to call them. But I'm smug about Cleveland, about this so-called Rust Belt full of people like me: first-generation college graduates whose lives are bigger and better because of parents who kept a promise that they would be the last to carry lunch pails to work.

When these are your roots, you're more likely to see a waitress or bartender as a human being. You can even name a relative who works in the same kind of job. You also feel an uneasy gratitude when you watch them work—wiping tables, juggling plates, and smiling at loutish customers—and see a future you managed to escape. Turns a tip into cause, which I discovered time and again in my years as a columnist for *The Plain Dealer*. Whenever I wrote about a restaurant boss taking unfair advantage of tipped employees, the reader response was swift, and overwhelmingly on the side of those hourly wage earners.

In Cleveland, if you tell readers that someone is mistreating workers just because he or she can, a lot of them are going to do something about it. They're going to tip big, and in cash. They're going to call managers, too, and threaten to tell all their friends about their lousy business practices if they don't change their ways. Most people in this region want to do the right thing, and there's an untapped power for change in that singular truth.

We are our stories, which is why I'm ever-faithful to this bruised and battered town. My own story begins with my parents, who raised their four kids in small-town Ashtabula but insisted that all roads worth traveling lead to Cleveland.

In our family, Cleveland was a city that kept its promises and emboldened lives. Anything related to Cleveland was bigger, bolder.

The Cleveland Electric Illuminating Company made my dad a hero in our house. For more than three decades, he worked in CEI's Ashtabula plant on Lake Erie's shore. We'd flick a switch and my mother would say, "Your daddy made that electricity." Before you laugh, imagine a six-year-old daughter's state of wonder as she stares at the ceiling light and pictures her father harnessing a bolt of lightning with his bare hands.

Ten years later, I was a 16-year-old cheerleader leaping into a cartwheel when I collapsed on the gym floor during a basketball game, gasping for air. I'd been sick for weeks, misdiagnosed with bronchitis. An ambulance rushed me to a nearby hospital. It was the first of many such scary asthma attacks, and long hospital stays for a disease out of control. After the third ambulance ride, our family doctor stood at the foot of my bed and said to my parents, "We've got to get her to Cleveland."

When I was admitted to the Cleveland Clinic in the early 1970s, my terrified parents finally allowed themselves to catch their own breaths. Doctors delivered cutting-edge treatment, and blew wide open my small-town view of the world. Before going to the Clinic, the only foreigner I'd ever met was a white South African student attending my high school through an international exchange program. Suddenly, I was meeting men and women from around the world. Some of my most enduring memories of that scary time in my life swirl around images of white coats, breathing chambers, and my father pacing as he strained to understand men with exotic accents promising that his daughter would one day run again.

I wish I remembered the name of the young Clinic resident who stopped by every morning to drop off a copy of *The Plain Dealer,* then returned at the end of the day to talk about some of the stories I'd read. Looking back, I can see that he was trying to distract me from the anxiety that was exacerbating my asthma, but it was so intoxicating to have an adult male—a doctor, no less!—listen to me as if I had something to say.

On the day I graduated from Kent State University, my mother wiped her eyes and said, "You aren't going to leave us, are you?" She knew I was weighing my only job offer, at a newspaper in Indiana. She also knew I'd never go if she wanted me to stay.

Old story, that one. I packed up and headed to Cleveland, just as I was raised to do. Eventually, at age 36, I landed at *The Plain Dealer.* It was my first and only full-time newspaper job.

If you work hard and get attention for what you do, you can get big ideas about your future and leave the place that built you. Certainly, there were moments when I—and friends who loved me—wondered if my career would be bigger and better somewhere else. Such ruminations are born of a self-importance that's bound to catch up with you. Single motherhood in my 30s was a real leveler for me. Cleveland forgave my unfaithful yearnings and pulled me through the toughest time of my life. By the time I became a columnist, I couldn't imagine living anywhere else.

Over the years, Clevelanders have had plenty of opinions about mine, but they've also made it clear that ours is a family argument. I'm grateful for the willingness of so many strangers to claim me, and I'm always trying not to let them down. Clevelanders are not shy about their expectations. One of my cherished possessions is a box full of cards and letters from readers who, on the biggest day of my career, wanted me to know they were (a) mighty proud and (b) worried that I might let the good news go to my head.

Roots matter. Without that tethering, we can lose our way, but it's also true that a tree grows only as high as its roots will allow.

For me, Cleveland has always been a place where branches tickle the sky.

Speak In Tongues

Denise Grollmus

It's a cliché at this point that all Midwesterners love to boast that we grew up in the sorts of towns "where you had to make your own fun." What they mean to say is: we lived and died by listening to and making music. In my case, it was mid-90s indie rock. When I was old enough to start traveling around the world, I discovered that this sort of fanaticism for underground music was particular to towns like Cleveland, Ohio—cloudy towns and poor towns like Manchester, England or Glasgow, Scotland. In 1978, Robert Christgau wrote that two of the reasons Clevelanders were so fanatical about punk rock was "the weather's not the best" and "there's nothing much to do." He also wrote that,

> musically, I think of Akron-Cleveland as one place . . . . Both have long borne the impress of a large white industrial working class that now faces the removal of rubber and steel manufacture to the South; both also support many corporate headquarters and a large managerial and professional class. Both suffered major race riots in the '60s. Both experienced intense counterculture conflicts as well. Most important for our purposes, both continued to pursue an unusually active relationship with rock and roll long after the music biz had established itself elsewhere. Ohio is a big place, of course, but it does seem to turn out more rock musicians than most big places.

Like all the other postindustrial, punk rock fourteen-year-olds who came before me, I dutifully copied into my calendar the dates of concerts, listed in the pages of *Cleveland Scene* and *Cleveland Free Times*, for both of which I eventually worked. Since most of the shows were almost always on school nights, I usually never made it to any of them. Instead, I'd sit in my bedroom in Akron, spinning the bands' 7"s over and over and over again, trying to imagine Mary Lou Lord or Excuse Seventeen playing onstage at The Grog Shop or The Euclid Tavern. For the most part, just knowing that these bands were playing 40 minutes away was enough.

There was one club, however, for which I frequently risked my parents' ire. At the time, there was no cooler club than Speak in Tongues. It was so underground, that not even the free weeklies offered listings for the abundance of shows they put on—more than 2,000 in their time. You always had to hear about a Speak in Tongues show through word of mouth, or visit The Bent Crayon, the record-store equivalent of Speak in Tongues, and check out the listings that John, the store owner, would scrawl onto a dry erase board behind the counter.

In Akron, for those of us who sported Sonic Youth T-shirts, deemed Weezer too mainstream, and traded tapes of Modest Mouse's first EP, Speak in Tongues was *the* place. We uttered its name with a profound reverence. Our eyes would grow wide in the parking lot of Firestone High School or the lunchroom of Our Lady of the Elms when someone would let the rest of us know that Rachel's Band was coming, or Love as Laughter, or Cleveland's own The Old Hearts Club would be playing. For Kent's Harriet the Spy, we'd all scrounge for rides from the kids with cars and nights off at our after-school jobs.

For me, it was a serious feat getting to Speak in Tongues. First, I had to lie. I would tell my mother that I was spending the night at Alison's house. Then, I'd have to convince Alison to drive me up to Cleveland with her, because Rocketship was my favorite band ever and I *had* to go, or I would die. Then, Alison would have to see if Mike would let us crash at his place in North Olmsted, because she didn't like driving back to Akron at two in the morning. Then, if it all fell together, we would prepare ourselves for a trip to Mecca in Alison's 1982 red Ford Escort, replete with shitty tape recordings of the latest album released by whatever band was playing—Joan of Arc, The Brian Jonestown Massacre, The Spiny Anteaters, The Frogs.

The club was located on Cleveland's West Side, at the corner of Lorain Avenue and West 44th Street. It was a dangerous neighborhood, where, more than once during a show, there was a shooting or a break in a few doors down, and as we waited for the headlining band to play, we'd watch as the Cleveland PD hung crime scene tape or we'd brave the walk down the street for $1 hot dogs.

Few people even knew the club was there. There were no signs, just an old storefront that appeared abandoned, with the exception of some Cleveland weirdo sitting on a stool against the front door, collecting the $8 or whatever it took to get inside. It was a total dive with worn out wood floors and sagging couches against the walls. Some said it was a bowling alley at one time, though I'm not sure if that was true. There was barely a stage or a PA system and the only incandescence came from the dim glow of Christmas lights haphazardly hanging from a sheet that hid the "backstage," which was little more than a narrow pathway cluttered with broken music equipment. It was the scariest, coolest place I'd ever been in my life. It was like living inside a Jim Jarmusch movie—gritty, dark, and sparsely populated. The sort of place you could only find in Cleveland.

Speak in Tongues had a bar, but no liquor license. Bands would set up their merch along the shelves usually reserved for bottles of booze. They'd hang their t-shirts along the empty beer taps and display their vinyl along the bar, and then they'd sit and wait on duct-taped bar stools so that you could mingle with them before the show, if you were brave enough to approach someone as awesome as Isaac Brock or as terrifying as Anton Newcombe. People who had the right sort of ID would go across the street to the shady gas station to buy six-packs of cheap beer and 40 ounces. Some would come back bloodied and bruised, jumped by local thugs. Still, they rarely called the cops or went to the hospital, refusing to miss the show.

The place was ran by a collective of guys who booked the shows, though Daniel "Big Dan" Santovin, a bespectacled and bearded skater and old school DIY punk rocker, was SIT's main fixture, the man who made it all run, at least during the years I went there. At that time, he lived in the basement with a few other revolving members and there was almost always a fresh liter of kittens that infested the crusty old couches in the main room with fleas. The rent was paid by the proceeds from shows and bands usually only made enough for gas money. Depending on the band playing, there could be anywhere from two people (Push Kings) or well over two hundred (June of 44). And there were the regular fixtures at every single show, like "Bleeding Earman," who I saw almost monthly for over five years, but whose real name I never learned. He was the scene's token weirdo—a middle-aged man who'd earned his nickname while he was shopping at The Bent Crayon and, in the middle of a conversation with the owner, his ear spontaneously started bleeding. For a while, he always wore a fluorescent fanny pack and matching painter's cap while he smoked cigars. The, he started playing his harmonica along with the bands, until he was threatened with being permanently banned. There was a year when he'd show up at SIT always wearing the same Confederate Army Jacket, before he started appearing in roller blades, his torso wrapped in Christmas lights and glow sticks. Almost always, you could find him passed out in a corner while his equally crazy girlfriend sipped god knows what from a water bottle and shouted obscenities at him.

I was usually the youngest of those in attendance, at least three years younger than the average age of SIT show-goers (unless Alison's younger sister came), a fact that made me as proud as it did insecure. I had a crush on every boy in the building, no matter how old, and I loved-hated the way people like Big Dan treated me like a little sister, always offering me advice on boys ("Never have sex. Sex makes people boring."), or introducing me to bands so I could give them the care packages I became notorious for bringing to shows—bags usually stuffed with loads of candy and glow-in-the-dark stars and mix tapes and at least one copy of my fanzine. Years later, I learned that I had earned a nickname, too. "Candy Girl."

Though I know I was there during the winter months, when I think of SIT, it's always oppressively hot in my memories. My memory of the Rocketship and Henry's Dress show is coated in sweat, all hazy with steam. We were the only ones there aside from four people who'd driven all the way from Toronto, Canada. I remember dancing my ass off to the point of passing out, my cargo shorts and baggy Beat Happening T-shirt doused in sweat, clinging to my body.

My other favorite memory is being there five years later with the boy that would become my husband and then my ex-husband. We fell in love through music and even one of our first dates was conducted during an Adult show at SIT, at a time when we had the right IDs to buy 40 ounces. It was also one of the last times I saw Steve, one of our best friends, at a show. Steve passed away from leukemia only a few years after that night, when we were all 23 years old. Eventually, my boyfriend and I started our own band, Churchbuilder, which, like most of the bands I ever saw at SIT, vanished inside of the same obscurity into which we were born. Our crowning achievement was booking a show at SIT. Again, all I remember is the stifling heat, Big Dan soaked in sweat with a big goofy grin on his face, like a proud dad, as he stood at the front of the stage with maybe a dozen other people, mostly our Akron friends, watching us. While we loaded the van, he gave us just enough to cover the gas money. I didn't know it at the time, but it would be my last time inside of Speak in Tongues.

V. Conflict

TONIGHT THE INAUGURAL PATROL FOR CLEVELAND'S NEWEST ALLY IN THE WAR ON CRIME FINDS OUR HERO DEEP IN THOUGHT OVER A FORMERLY UNCONSIDERED RAMIFICATION OF HIS NEWFOUND ABILITIES.

DON'T KNOW WHAT IT'S GONNA TAKE TO ADMINISTER A PROPER *BUZZ* ANYMORE. GUESS FOLKS'LL JUST THINK I'M AN ALKIE.

ACQUIRING THAT OLD *APAMA* ANIMAL SPIRIT HAS ENHANCED MY TASTE BUDS. IT MAKES MOST OF WHAT I DRINK TASTE LIKE *GUTTER SWILL*, BUT THIS *DORT* ALE --

ACES HIGH.

WITH EACH PASSING ROUND ILYIA GROWS MORE IMPATIENT.

MAN, I'M JONESIN' FOR SOME *ACTION* ALREADY. MAYBE I NEED TO DRUM IT UP *MYSELF!*

CREESH

THE NEWS KEEPS HARPING ON THE *CRIME* PROBLEM, BUT I'M NOT SEEING IT.

EVERYONE LOOKS PRETTY FRIGGIN' HAPPY.

AS HE STARES AT THE HIPSTERS, SCENESTERS, AND LOVERS A CONFUSION SETS IN. HE WONDERS WHAT IT *IS* THAT HE'S REALLY PROTECTING.

Harvey Pekar's Nagging Muse

Erick Trickey

Harvey Pekar—*the grouch, the pessimist, the quitter*—wrote about the Cleveland that really was, not the Cleveland we aspire to be. He debuted his underground comic book *American Splendor* in 1976, seven years after the Cuyahoga River last caught fire and two years before the city's default. With *American Splendor*'s tagline, "From off the streets of Cleveland comes . . . ." Pekar used the city's "mistake on the lake" reputation to launch his literary persona: the heroic anti-hero.

Cleveland animated Harvey Pekar's work. Home was his recurring subject, his nagging muse, his alter ego. More than any other Cleveland writer, Pekar personified his hometown. "The city started to decline," he wrote in his posthumous book *Harvey Pekar's Cleveland*. "So did my luck."

A frustrated athlete, college dropout, moody lover, and self-doubting artist, Pekar had a self-esteem problem before Cleveland's raged. His memoir *The Quitter* recounted his bitterness at his own mediocrity, his unwillingness to stick with a sport he was merely good at. His short temper sabotaged him until he lowered his expectations and accepted the stability of his famously unfamous VA file clerk job. Only then, in his late 30s, did he find his artistic medium and creative breakthrough.

Inspired by his friend Robert Crumb and other creators of underground comics, he made the unlikely transition from jazz critic to comic book writer. His aversion to superhero comics compelled him to explore their opposite. He decided that his life, or anyone's, could be art if observed and rendered with insight, wit and an ear for dialogue.

"Ordinary life is pretty complex stuff," he declared. That theme resonated more deeply because it came from the streets and porches of Cleveland, not our endlessly celebrated capitals of creative class culture.

Pekar died in 2010. Two years later, writers, thinkers, and artists in the Great Lakes states are embracing the remnants of our cities' boomtown glories, finding meaning in the struggle to respond to our economic decline, and creating something new from what's left. This "Rust Belt Chic" movement is an attempt to finally prove that the factory coast actually has a distinct culture.

A lot of people don't believe that, including people from the Rust Belt. They think we're the norm, the people with no regional culture, the people who sound like the people on TV. We're flyover country. The place talented people used to be from. The place with no "there" there.

Decades ago, Pekar's work was already refuting the idea of the Rust Belt as a non-culture. Like today's Rust Belt artists, he was fascinated by the city's ethnic heritage, fluent in the history recorded in their grand architecture, obsessed with a sense of loss and ruin. But there's one very important difference between him and his enthusiastic Rust Belt chic successors: Pekar's view of Cleveland and the Rust Belt was almost entirely devoid of optimism. In fact, Pekar was a gloomy man. I discovered that right away when I interviewed him and his wife, Joyce Brabner, in the fall of 2003. *American Splendor*, the biopic about Pekar's life and comics career, had just made Pekar the everyman hero of indie cinema, but the experience had failed to dent his permanent frown.

"This was kind of an exceptional time for me, a diverting time," he told me, his huge, dark eyebrows in full weedy bloom. He was "kinda depressed" it was ending, since he had to hustle for writing jobs again. Maybe the movie would help, he allowed. "Then I'll be happy," he said—and caught himself. "At least as happy as I get, which is not too happy."

I respected that. Pekar's gloom gave him an artist's vision of Cleveland, like a painter going through a lifelong gray period. His realist's eye caught something about the town by focusing on his monotonous job, his favorite cheap restaurants, his bohemian's taste for jazz and klezmer.

Over breakfast in a diner, cartoon Harvey chatted about the yuppies moving into Ohio City, driving up rents. Telling a story about his family, he looked up at a two-story double house and told his readers how Cleveland was once filled with big families who'd share a home—two sisters, for instance, and their husbands and kids, one on each floor. His collage of West Side Market images showed the characters, the crowds, and the hucksterism of the vendors.

"Ever see anything prettier?" one asked, holding a handful of cherries out to the reader.

Historians and sociologists must envy Pekar's penetrating observations of how regular people lived and experienced Cleveland's massive social changes over the last 70 years, as well as his understanding of how neighborhoods developed reputations and captured imaginations. The best parts of *Harvey Pekar's Cleveland,* for instance, follow him on strolls through neighborhoods he's known: Cleveland's Southeast Side in his youth, the lost '60s bohemia at Euclid and East 105th, Coventry's evolution from the '70s to today.

His social commentary is especially strong when it turns to Cleveland's race relations. Though bullied as a kid for being one of the few whites left in his neighborhood, he remained curious about black experience all his life, rejecting cynical withdrawal but also avoiding easy idealism and feel-good buzzwords. Both sides of the divide have done each other harm, he insisted, but we can and ought to do better. One scene in *Harvey Pekar's Cleveland* seems especially prescient: He walks his beloved Coventry Road, angrily defending multiracial Cleveland Heights's reputation from the fears of some whites. Pekar wrote the scene about a year before the 2011 "flash mob" controversy, when the city imposed a strict youth curfew on Coventry and Lee roads to deter gatherings of several hundred black teens. His loyalty to Cleveland Heights reads even more powerfully and poignantly now.

In an *American Splendor* comic from the '80s, Pekar tags along on a sightseeing tour for a visiting writer that included the steel mills and the Orthodox church where *The Deer Hunter* was filmed. But the grandeur of St. Theodosius did not inspire him to swooning hopes of civic rebirth.

"Boy, Cleveland really seems like it's dying," he lamented.

He never wavered from that judgment. After Mayor George Voinovich's 1980s "Comeback City" vision realigned the city's politics and social debate, Pekar became the literary voice of the anti-boosters. His pessimism led him to mistrust the comeback stories Cleveland tells itself. He refused to visit the Rock and Roll Hall of Fame and mocked the painted-face Dawg Pound crowd that celebrated the Cleveland Browns' return.

When I met him, Jane Campbell, then mayor, had just dissed him. He'd written a *New York Times* op-ed cartoon in response to the August 2003 electrical blackout, which had started in Northeast Ohio and spread across several states.

"Once again, they're laughing at my hometown," it began. The op-ed lamented Cleveland's Rust Belt plight, the loss of people and industrial jobs. "An air of depression pervades the city," Pekar wrote.

He warned that America ignored the troubles of cities like Cleveland and Detroit at its own peril. But his gloom had left the mayor peeved.

"There's a lot more going on than Harvey Pekar seems to know," Campbell sniped.

"Harvey's been attacked for that for years," Brabner told me. She recalled his cranky late-night jousts on *Late Night with David Letterman.*

"Harvey, how are things in Cleveland?" Letterman asked him once.

"What aspect of Cleveland life are you particularly interested in, Dave?" Pekar asked, his voice lilting with sarcasm. "The climate? The unemployment situation, perhaps?"

Afterward, civic boosters asked Pekar why he hadn't raved about the new Jacobs Field.

"There are people who like me to talk about Cleveland the way it is and be honest," he explained.

Exactly. Pekar had to be relentlessly unsentimental to achieve his art: seeing Cleveland's essence in everyday life.

Pekar would likely have scoffed at any enthusiastic use of the phrase "Rust Belt Chic." He was the opposite of chic. The term could only have applied to him in the most ironic way.

In fact, his wife, Joyce Brabner, likely coined the phrase in a 1995 interview. She wasn't talking about local pride, but about New Yorkers' condescending tendency to reduce Midwestern culture to kitschy stereotype."

Yet eight years later, the *American Splendor* filmmakers showed that out-of-towners could understand Pekar and the Rust Belt in a deeper way. They took Pekar's wintry vision and let just a little sunlight in, distilling his marriage to Brabner into a misfits' love story and casting a lover's eye on the misfit city. Shooting in Cleveland and Lakewood, the filmmakers discovered the town's character in little bakeries and diners and brick apartment buildings, spots unchanged since at least the 1970s. Perhaps the most poignant, haunting scene in the film comes when actor Paul Giamatti recites Pekar's "Who Is Harvey Pekar?" monologue, an existential reflection prompted by finding other Harvey Pekars in the phone book. During part of the monologue, Giamatti paces in front of an aging brick warehouse or factory as snow falls. The post-industrial emptiness of the backdrop reflects his yearning for meaning. Like Pekar's comics, the movie made Cleveland's distinctiveness fascinating and metaphoric long before the current Rust Belt buzz.

I doubt Pekar would ever have entertained more than a faint hope that embracing Rust Belt culture would lead to an economic revival. He'd seen too much to put faith in that. His work stands as a warning to the next generation of creative Rust Belt residents: an artistic embrace of one's home can lose its artistry and honesty if it slides into sunny cheerleading.

Instead of accepting optimism as a civic duty, Pekar celebrated Cleveland's distinctiveness while confronting its problems. He rejected boosterism but embraced stubborn loyalty.

Gary Snyder's line about the Clevelandness of '60s poet d. a. levy describes Pekar too: "His hometown, Cleveland, that he wouldn't move from. Like the Sioux warriors who tied themselves to a spear and stuck it in the ground, never to retreat."

The end of the story is written in the last pages of *Harvey Pekar's Cleveland:* the writer settling into retirement in a place where triumphant moments are fleeting and happy endings elusive—in other words: home.

—Portions of this essay first appeared in Cleveland Magazine

South Euclid, Then and Now

Afi-Odelia E. Scruggs

An old-fashioned letter inspires our writer to ask what has kept her suburban neighborhood strong since it was built 50 years ago and why, despite its challenges, she believes it will stay strong for 50 more.

D *ear Afi-Odelia:*
    I am a 55-year-old Jewish woman who grew up in Cleveland and now lives in Canada. I saw your article on interviewing your grandmother this morning and it was right on target with my own thoughts of the past few years . . . .

The real reason I'm writing is that all of my childhood memories and wellsprings of deep feeling are tied up in a house . . . in South Euclid . . . I was in Cleveland several times over the past ten years . . . and every time I would park out in front of that house. Once or twice I rang the bell, but no one ever answered. Probably better that way . . . .

But the connection is so strong for me that I Googled you and found your Web site with your picture on it. This may sound strange to you but you look kind of like me.

Well, that's all. I never write letters like this. But I just wanted to say hello—who knows, maybe you know the house I'm talking about. All my memories are in the late '50s and through the '60s, lovely years of peace and quiet on Wrenford Road.

Wishing you the same.

Fern

Getting a letter is rare these days, perhaps because we write for the moment, not for generations. But Fern had sent me a letter—even though it was delivered by e-mail. The emotion behind her words evoked a time when folks committed their thoughts to fine stationery. Her words made me recall the thrill of opening an envelope and rubbing a sheet of heavy writing paper between my fingers. I even became wistful for the task of deciphering handwriting.

She'd responded to an article I'd written about digitizing an interview with my 92-year-old grandmother. The process, like Fern's e-mail, straddled the gap between then and now. The interview was on tape, and I was converting it to an MP3. The article appeared in an online magazine, not in print.

Through our computers, Fern and I had recaptured pieces of our pasts.

I know her old home because I pass it daily: I'm only six blocks away on Bexley Boulevard. The house is white with white awnings. The lawn is the shade of green that comes from regular weekends spent applying fertilizer and weed killer. It's not much different from other houses on the block.

I wouldn't have even noticed it, except for Fern's letter.

After I read it, I got up from the computer and went downstairs. I sat in my living room and gazed out the big picture window for a while. I looked at my street, trying to see what about it would have moved Fern to write once she found me.

My house was built in 1954, a boom time for many suburbs, including South Euclid. The town became a destination for Jewish and Italian families. The GI Bill put homeownership within the grasp of a generation, so they left the cities, flowing onto streets like mine.

There's not much architectural variation around here, just a bungalow and a driveway, one after the other. On one, the entrance faces the street. On the next, the entrance faces sideways, toward the neighboring house. Awnings provide the only color. Malvina Reynolds could have been talking about Bexley Boulevard when she bemoaned the "little boxes made of ticky tacky . . . little boxes all the same."

This neighborhood is a relic.

My brother confirmed that opinion when he visited from Tennessee this summer. He stood in my front lawn and looked at the houses neatly lining the street. On that day, Cleveland's fickle weather was behaving itself. The sky was as bold and blue as a robin's egg. The wispy clouds looked like ribbons in a little girl's hair.

Everyone was out. The neighbors were filling the flower beds with impatiens and begonias or spreading mulch. The teenage girls were strolling toward the park, surreptitiously looking for boys. The cheers from a softball game floated over the fence and hovered over my yard.

My brother walked to the tree lawn, turned east, then west, then walked back to my side door.

"This looks like *Leave It to Beaver*," he said.

He wasn't being sarcastic. He was being complimentary. He wasn't talking about the homogeneity; he was talking about the feeling that this neighborhood had been here for 50 years and would be here 50 or 60 more. That longevity blended with the languid vitality of a summer weekend to create a scene made for black-and-white sitcoms.

Of course, a lot has changed since Fern's lovely years of peace and quiet on Wrenford Road.

I've seen two of the original residents die, while others moved to more manageable apartments. When I arrived in 1995, I was the only black person on my part of the block. Now, three of my neighbors are black, and I often see groups of African American children walking home from school.

The shift has some residents—themselves black—complaining that the neighborhood has "gone down." Of course, that's long been a code phrase for newcomers who aren't the same color or class as the established residents.

To me, the challenge doesn't have to do with race or class—it's about the town's financial health. Still, I understand my neighbors' fears. Cleveland is an area made up of ethnic and racial enclaves, and many of those divides still haven't been bridged.

But some good may come out of my neighbors' reactions to change. Some of the streets have formed block clubs because, so they say, crime is becoming a problem. Others go door-to-door, introducing themselves and handing out invitations to block meetings in the park. It's a way, a lady once told me, for us to get to know one another. They may be acting out of fear, but they're still building a community.

In his book *The Levittowners,* sociologist Herbert Gans described the way a suburban development changed from long blocks of nearly identical houses to a complex network of friends and cliques, of organizations and alliances. One observation stayed on my mind.

"The residents had at first associated almost exclusively with their neighbors, but . . . some had sought more compatible people and activities outside the block . . . and had set in motion the founding of community-wide groups," Gans wrote back in 1967.

According to Gans, a neighborhood was a block of residences. But my neighborhood stretches from Mayfield Road on the north to Cedar Road on the south, from Warrensville Center Road on the east to Belvoir Boulevard on the west. I define my neighborhood not by the proximity, but by the people I know who live within walking distance. As friends moved in, my conception of my neighborhood expanded. And as I met more people, I became part of something more: the community. Obviously, a community transcends a neighborhood, but the character of a neighborhood determines the character of the community. In mine, the fact that families still walk home from the swimming pool in the park—amenities that lured hundreds of thousands to Levittown and developments like it—sends a message: This is a safe place; this is a family place; this is an enduring place.

That doesn't mean the future is assured. "Elmwood," an urban planner who posts to SkyscraperCity.com, calls South Euclid "a low-profile, mid-century suburb on the edge."

"South Euclid is emerging as a hotspot for foreclosures; the number is increasing and there's a growing inventory of vacant houses," he wrote in January 2007. "While real estate prices are rising outside the city line, they've flat-lined in South Euclid."

When Elmwood listed my town's strengths—it has good schools and good public services and it seems to be handling integration well, without much white flight—my thoughts returned to Fern.

She lived in the neighborhood when times were flush, and her memories reflect that optimism and prosperity.

I'm here as the community peers into an uncertain future. I understand that anxiety, of course. But I also see things I didn't see until Fern's letter opened my eyes: the tranquility of a Sunday afternoon, when young parents push strollers that look like cars while toddlers play at steering and share the sidewalks with couples walking hand in hand, getting a little exercise in the cooling day.

—Originally published in Cleveland Magazine

Toward a Literature of the Rust Belt

Christine Borne Nickras

T he title of this essay is taken from Mark Winegardner's afterword to *Good Roots: Writers Reflect on Growing Up in Ohio.* Winegardner, author of *Crooked River Burning,* the only epic novel about 20th century Cleveland you'll ever need to read, was duly skeptical about whether anyone would buy the idea that there was such a thing as Midwestern literature, even though five of the nine American Nobel Prize winners in literature have been from the Midwest.

Likewise, I'm not sure this essay belongs in an anthology of Rust Belt Chic, a concept I associate with the kind of bar where you can order a hot dog with SpaghettiOs on it while a twentysomething in a fake beard spins his grandpa's Jimmy Sturr records. Reading is not chic and never will be, even though prancing about in an indie bookstore with a microbrew in your fist and proclaiming your love for Bukowski will apparently never go out of style. But as you have purchased this book, I am hopeful that you might purchase other books, possibly the ones mentioned herein.

As an enthusiastic wearer of acetate spandex blends and incorrigible hoarder of Arby's coupons, I am probably not qualified to talk about chic either. But I am qualified to talk about Rust Belt literature. In September 2010, I founded *The Cleveland Review: A Journal of Rust Belt Literature* with my co-editors Katheryn Norris, Camilla Grigsby and Wells Addington. We did this to highlight work currently produced in this region, which extends from Pittsburgh to Buffalo, Cleveland to South Bend to Detroit, and any city or town in the Upper Midwest that's known more for what it used to make than what it makes now. We're also keen on reading works from our sizable expat community, those lucky creatures who have decamped for the coasts and made something of themselves or died trying.

Since then I have read hundreds of short stories, poems, and essays with the postindustrial Midwest as the backdrop or theme. Rust Belt literature is about more than just gruff steelworkers with hearts of gold, or feeling sad about abandoned factories as you drive past them on the freeway, perhaps from your loft apartment in a gentrifying neighborhood to your job at some kind of "creative group" at an office park in the suburbs. Rust Belt literature is surely the story of the decline of the middle class, the story of blue-collar people who have less and less of a place in the world that they and their fathers (and mothers) literally built. It is the story of the sons and daughters of Irish or Eastern European immigrants and the story of the Great Migration, about Muslim Americans and their place in country still seized by Islamophobia, about what happens when people don't use cities like they're cities anymore. Rust Belt literature answers the question: What is it like to live on a street where all the other houses are abandoned but yours? What is it like to survive on raccoon meat and the purslane that grows out of the cracks in your sidewalk because the nearest grocery store is twenty miles away and you don't have a car? It is the cautionary tale of an empire that's fallen and the citizens who don't believe it (and those who do). Rust Belt literature is the story of all the problems in America writ small, it is the realization that positive thinking alone won't reverse decades of corruption, economic devastation, and apathy.

Within this context, a few clear themes emerge in the study of Rust Belt fiction:

American Dream in Ruins: This theme is parallel to the Lost Cause of the Confederacy found in Southern literature. As a story, *Gone With the Wind* shares many of the same characteristics as *Crooked River Burning*. It starts out in an improbably idyllic time that you watch uncomfortably because you know it's going to end. There's an equally doomed romance to keep an eye on. Both stories are filled with a dizzying array of historical details, including the racism of the times. Like *Gone With the Wind*, *Crooked River Burning* focuses on that tenuous period between

155

the death of one era and the birth of another: in this case, the period between the birth of the middle class and its subsequent breakdown, the period that Rust Belters look back on with as much problematic nostalgia as Lost Cause Southerners looked back upon the Confederacy.

This idea is also captured in Bonnie Jo Campbell's short story "The Inventor, 1972," in which a horribly maimed hunter, injured as a young man in a steel mill accident and living as a hermit ever since, hits a young girl walking alone alongside a foggy road. As she lies bleeding on the ground, she sees her whole future in ruins: "No one sings songs about one-legged girls." The outrage is palpable: this wasn't supposed to happen. Everything was supposed to be perfect, or at least perfect according to the modest and reasonable way you imagined it: you grow up, get a job (or a husband), buy a house, and retire at 65.

Impending Doom—And What to Do About It: The lessons imparted by the fall of American industry aren't totally lost on inhabitants of the Rust Belt: Bonnie Jo Campbell's "World of Gas" and "Fuel for the Millennium" (anthologized in *American Salvage*) both feature characters in the process of hoarding supplies for Y2K. They might appear ridiculous in their preparations for the techno-apocalypse, but they acknowledge that life goes on after a disaster. In *The Keepers of Truth*, Michael Collins suggests that the postindustrial economy is a woman's economy. While Bill and his boss, Ed, rhapsodize about how far the town has fallen, Ed's wife Darlene has started a thriving glamor photography business, offering an add-on service called "Car Theft": for a price, Darlene and her employees will "steal" your husband's car and have it vacuumed, polished, and waxed while he remains none the wiser. The idea being, of course, that the pride he feels at having a like-new vehicle will have a trickle-down effect in the marriage.

Rust as Decay—Or Metamorphosis: Billy Poe, the young protagonist in Philipp Meyer's *American Rust*, frequently goes hunting amid the ruins of the shuttered steel mill near his hometown of Buell, Pennsylvania. Billy notes that although Buell is recovering economically, it will never compare to what it used to be. This bothers the older generation, but having grown up completely within the postindustrial period, it doesn't bother him. Rust Belt is all he knows, and as an enthusiast of the natural world he takes heart in the fact that nature has transformed the grounds of the steel mill into a fine habitat for animals and native plants. This brings to mind a 2004 story from *This American Life*, in which a Brooklyn musician transforms his Hasidic friend Chaim into an underground rock star. They decide to call him Curly Oxide, owing to Chaim's rust-colored payots, and because oxidation (i.e., rust) represents one thing changing into another thing.

Return of the Prodigal Expat: In Michael Collins' *The Keepers of Truth*, Bill, a reporter for the *Daily Truth*, has returned home to the once-thriving town in downstate Illinois where his grandfather had singlehandedly built a now-defunct refrigerator manufacturing empire. Although Bill attempts to use his position to pontificate on the decline of the American Dream, he is expected to report exclusively on local bake-offs, high school football rivalries, and eventually the brutal murder of Ronny Lawton's father.

The question that preys most heavily on the reader's mind, however, is not "Who killed Ronny Lawton's father?" but "Why on Earth did Bill leave Chicago and move back to this awful place?" The answer is not because he failed at law school. Nor did Bill labor under any noble illusion of reversing the town's hard luck and bringing it back to its glorious heyday. The answer is more complicated. Although Bill hates this place, he's drawn back to it out of a debilitating sense of familial guilt: if he did not come home, there wouldn't be anyone to witness the death of the place his grandfather built (and which drove his father to suicide). If Bill did not return, no one would be around to observe that without any meaningful work to do, Rust Belt people were trapped and purposeless.

A similar theme arises in Scott Lasser's *Say Nice Things About Detroit*, whose title is taken from a 1970s-era booster campaign. After half a lifetime away, aging Gen X-er David Halpert flees from personal devastation (divorce and the death of a child) to his equally devastated hometown of Detroit. Though David experiences more of a redemption than Collins' protagonist, he is still plagued by the doubts of his friends, family and coworkers: What's wrong with you, that you would move back to Detroit?

So are we headed toward a literature of the Rust Belt? I hope so. I hope that the $400,000 advance Philipp Meyer received for *American Rust*, the selection of Bonnie Jo Campbell's *American Salvage* as National Book Award finalist in 2009, the choice of Detroit-born Philip Levine as 2011 US Poet Laureate, and the renewed interest in our regional culture will establish Rust Belt literature as an important genre in the American canon.

Of course, we'll probably fuck it up somehow. At the end of his afterword to *Good Roots*, Mark Winegardner laments that Midwestern literature will never be a recognized genre like Southern literature because in our "sausage-fingered hands" any attempt at regional identity will only ever come off as boosterism. Actually what I'm afraid of is not that Rust Belt literature would come off as boosterism but that it would get eclipsed by it: I'm concerned that any author who manages to tell the ugly side of the Rust Belt story will find him- or herself suddenly unwelcome in their own hometown, like Sinclair Lewis was after *Main Street*, never mind that the work earned him a Nobel Prize. And we'll just be stuck doing what we've been doing for the last two generations: sending our thinkers, artists and philosophers away, crowing all the while about how cheap it is to live here.

Dangerous Poets

Nicole Hennessy

In the 1960s, Cleveland devoured its poets. The city's obedient officials lunged at language, seething with paranoid visions of poetry. Freedom. Silence. Obscenity. Among these poets was Tom Kryss. Though, if you ask him, he'll tell you he was merely on the fringes of the turbulent literary scene.

"What was the literary scene?" he asks. "A bunch of coffee houses? I never went to a coffee house."

Under the imprints Ghost Press, Cold Mountain Press and Black Rabbit Press, Tom published poets such as Douglas Blazek, Kent Taylor, Al Purdy, Howard McCord, and D. R. Wagner. He relished the physical act of putting books together, taking great care to make them aesthetically appealing. For him, bookmaking was an art form. A book, in the technical sense, contains words between covers. But these pamphlet-like manifestations spoke for themselves. They screamed at the people of Cleveland who, for the most part, sought to repress their reactions by allowing authority to keep them safe from their daydreams. Printing books was fun, but it became increasingly dangerous.

Reading the newspaper, on July 15, 1966, Tom came across an article—"Small-Cause Champ Can't Fight Effect"—about an "erstwhile underground leader of a concrete and social comment poetry movement in Northern Ohio," d.a. levy. The article mentioned that his work could be found at a bookstore downtown. Intrigued, Tom got on the bus and headed to the Asphodel Bookstore, which was located in the Old Arcade.

The Asphodel wasn't just an ordinary bookshop. *The New York Times'* bestsellers didn't stand a chance among its printed revolutions of mind and spirit. And Jim Lowell wasn't just an ordinary bookseller. He was as prolific in Cleveland as the writers of the books themselves, and was gaining a reputation as one of the most important book dealers and collectors the United States, if not the entire world.

On the Arcade's fourth floor, beneath Cleveland sky pouring in through a glass ceiling, Tom found himself situated within a small, hole-in-the-wall store lined with books. Near the window was a rack dedicated to local writers, which was dominated by d.a.'s work—books he had self-published under imprints such as 7 Flowers Press and Renegade Press. Tom began to riffle through them, accumulating a small stack. When he was satisfied with his selections, he went to pay for them, his teenage hands gripping their flesh. He had never seen books like these. They were just as artful as the poetry and prose contained inside. The stack hadn't amounted to more than $10, and he gladly handed Jim the cash.

In his spare time, Tom began frequenting the Asphodel. The article he had read about d.a. implied that the poet was living on less than $1 a day and was concerned about how he would continue printing. Working in the storeroom of the Polyclinic Hospital, Tom would steal food and reams of mimeograph paper. "Here, give these to d.a., Jim, he needs this," Tom said, leaving boxes of supplies in the shop.

"There was in those days some sense of gratitude when a ream of paper fell into the hands. From the facial expressions, the effervescence of the recipient, you would think the worth of the tightly wrapped package much greater than five hundred sheets," Tom once wrote. "There was also an idea, then extant, that the remission of black ink into the paper turned the paper into gold. The words themselves may have had something to do with this; but the mimeograph's spillages, entirely accidental it seems, had the same effects on the mind of the printer."

Sitting in his trailer in Ravenna, Ohio, Tom remembers these and other things. His face twinges slightly as he does so, and two deep wrinkles meander across his forehead, his palm pressing up against them as he runs his fingers through his grey hair. Each thought he has about printed matter prompts him to extract evidence from the literary black hole in the back of his trailer, where neatly packed on shelves are books from all over the world, the plastic protecting them denoting their worth.

It's been a long time since the publication of *Book of Rabbits*—a wordless compilation of the screenprinted creatures which would sometimes run in d.a.'s newspaper, *The Buddhist Third Class Junkmail Oracle*. Still, staring out from the pages of a new edition, they remain unchanged by decades.

There is a hobo rabbit. There is a rabbit afraid of its own shadow wafting into a somewhat distant room. There are rabbits entrapped by predisposed presumptions, contentedly shipwrecked rabbits, and starry-eyed rabbits that sit atop Mount Rushmore, enveloped in the sun. There is one backward-glancing its reflection in a puddle steadily gathering water so as to prolong the mirage. Then, there's the last one, the one Tom always seems to come back to. Sitting at the base of a Romanesque column, it rests with a hint of a smile.

It is hard to measure a lifetime of making things appear as if from thin air, reproducing them and encouraging people to take interest, but Tom tries, considering the question, "Why am I doing this?"

After a lot of long pauses, he finally says, "There is no reason to be doing this and perhaps that's the best reason of all: to give so much time and energy to a pursuit that cannot be justified."

"That doesn't sound right either though, I don't know," he adds, changing his mind.

Things like poetry and drawings reasonably fall under the classification of art, Tom's sure. But as they are happening, it's not art, it's something else. It's an expression of a vague inner light, maybe. The best creations need no reason.

—*This story was excepted from Nicole Hennessy's self-published book,*
Black Rabbit

Not a Love Letter

Jimi Izrael

C *leveland is a cheap town* that ran out of good ideas in the '70s, and is now slapping down a casino and a medical mall in hopes of saving itself from falling into the lake. That casino will become a haven for hookers, robbers, robbing hookers, and people of color losing their paychecks on a lunchtime crap-out. Later, it will make a nice swap meet. Medical Mart is the next Galleria, because what we need is more Dollar Stores in a centralized location. I can't stand Cleveland, but I can't run too far away.

I have never, ever met any single person of color with any great passion for this city. Most black folks I know, if not chained to an under-paying, soulless vocation selling widgets and/or pierogi, get on the first thing leaving—at the very first chance. They come back for births, barbecues, and funerals, or sometimes they don't come back at all. Most of the Cleveland lovers are white, half-monied, often tethered to the city by some financial interest, and more than a few are invested in giving the city any variety of media handjobs. They wear tee shirts and tattoos, tributes to Cleveland. Those people are insane.

The truth?

Cleveland is a cruel and unforgiving place to creatives, people of color, and dreamers of any kind. There are fleeting moments of profound happiness to be found here, but mostly Cleveland has been awful to me and people who look like me. You can't make anything really special happen in the Midwestern malaise that is Cleveland, Ohio. And that isn't likely to change. You think it'll change—you think you can BE the change. Good for you, Skippy.

You are wrong.

I love Cleveland—she holds everything that is dear to me. But I avoid her, if I can. She has the public email and an old number that goes straight to voicemail. She's too earnest for an affection I cannot return. I love Cleveland because I have to: She is that old, skanky ex-GF who's nice enough but past her prime, wearing Chic jeans 10 years too small and door-knocker earrings, selling Mary Kay from the trunk of her '84 Camry, living for "Line Dance Nite." She's single and can't figure out why. Can't understand why I don't want to get back with her, because she's got it all going on: interviewing for night manager at Popeye's, about halfway through the same three associates degrees she's been working on since the '80s. She's got potential, drive and a weave she's paying for "on time." Together, we could be so hot, she says. Why can't we hook it back up? Why can't we stay together?

Yeah. I love Cleveland like that. Like. Umm. It's always so nice chatting. But I just came to see my kids. And now? Now I gotta go.

And no makeup, no hair weaves, no designer jeans or tattoos are likely to change that. She's a nasty chick on the front end of a gambling problem without a clue. Reluctant family that I'd deny if I could, but I can't.

She's my baby mama.

VI. Music

Bob Perkowski

The Tiny Record Empire in Cleveland

Laura Putre

T *here's only one Berry Gordy,* but Rust Belt America in the 1960s and '70s was also home to at least a handful of African-American-run recording studios that thrived without bank loans, relying on second-hand equipment, the owners' technical skill and ingenuity, and the ability to stretch a buck.

The proprietors of these studios were people like Thomas Boddie of Cleveland's Boddie Recording Company, who didn't dream big—unless dreaming big meant having your wife help lay cement in your backyard so you could build an addition on the garage for a record pressing plant.

Or driving around the country to church conventions, where you recorded preachers with a flat glass microphone you designed and built yourself mand your wife got arthritis in her knuckles from running the cassette tape duplication machine over and over, making 16 cassettes every three minutes, so you could sell $7 cassettes to 12,000 of the faithful.

"Boddie took baby steps and built himself a tiny little empire," says Rob Sevier, co-founder of Numero Group, a Chicago record label that specializes in archival recordings of obscure regional music, much of it soul, funk, and folk. A lot of the music Boddie recorded was junk—"tedious white gospel quartets," says Sevier, but there was plenty of great stuff in the heap, too.

Collectively, the recordings mothballed in the Boddies' backyard studio, sealed up from the time of Boddie's death from a brain aneurysm in 2007 until 2009, are a musical anthropologist's dream come true, telling the story of a lively regional music scene that might otherwise have been lost to history. They include hundreds of noteworthy regional acts, from traveling soul groups to Appalachian country-western acts that performed live but rarely got played on the radio, let alone scored a hit record. A few standouts achieved modest regional acclaim among soul fans: A. C. Jones, Creations Unlimited, the Inner Circle, Harvey and the Phenomenals, Jackie Russell, the Chantals.

"We weren't trying to be another Motown or any of these things because we couldn't afford it," says Louise Boddie, Thomas's wife and business partner. "We didn't have the kind of sponsors that Motown had. Our intent was just to record talent and lease it out to other companies who could afford to sponsor them."

Occasionally, if they thought someone might strike hitmaking gold, they would send the recording to a big-name studio. "If they liked it, then they would buy their contract," says Louise.

It took Sevier and Dante Carfagna, a DJ and curator of the Ohio Soul Recordings website, four years to get the Boddie family to agree to let Numero Group go through their archives and ultimately release a Boddie Recording Company compilation. "He was a tough nut to crack," says Sevier. He had sent Thomas Boddie selections from Numero's back catalog, but Boddie apparently was underwhelmed. "He was impressed with the packaging, but he had some negative things to say about the original music. Not about the mastering. He felt like the music wasn't very good, and he wasn't very open. He'd say things like, 'We've got some stuff going on. It's going to be another few months.' He kept pushing it back."

In 2006, through an obituary, Carfagna learned of Boddie's death. Sevier waited a couple of months, then called Boddie's still-grief-wracked wife, Louise. "She said, 'Why don't you call me back in a year?'" Sevier recalls. "A year went by, and I called again, and she wanted another year."

In late 2008, Louise Boddie agreed to the project. "The basic point was that on the cover would be a photo of Thomas," says Sevier. "This is his legacy."

Over the years, Boddie had been courted by a couple of British labels who were interested in licensing a handful of tracks, "but nothing of the scope we were talking about. I think everybody else who was interested had long since given up."

When the Numero guys finally cracked open the door to the backyard cinder-block studio, "it was like entering King Tut's tomb," wrote Numero co-founder Ken Shipley on a Numero Group blog in 2011. "A virtually untouched picture of what a real live '60s soul studio looked like."

Finally released in 2011, the *Boddie Recording Company* project turned out to be Numero Group's biggest yet, consisting of two booklets crammed with photographs of the studio, artists, and Boddie ephemera; two soul and r&b discs; one gospel disc, and a disc of tracks that didn't even make it to record.

"There's incredible music there," Sevier says of mining the unreleased material. Much of it is unlabeled. "The best way to identify artists is to bring a CD along when we meet people [who recorded at the studios], play the CD, and see if they recognize anything. It's a long and slow process."

Boddie didn't discriminate. He recorded whatever people would pay him to record. Cantors at Temple Tifereth-Israel on Cleveland's East Side. The O'Jays at a then-popular African-American club called Leo's Casino. Country-western acts up from West Virginia to perform at the First Baptist Church on Cleveland's Near West Side. All told, he had seven labels, two of which he curated—Soul Kitchen and Luau.

More of an electronics whiz than a musical one (though he loved jazz especially and was a big Stan Getz fan), after graduating second in his class from Cleveland's East Technical High School, Boddie found work as a Baldwin organ repairman. According to Louise, the white-run piano company where he applied for the job at first didn't want to hire him "because they didn't know how people would receive him as a man of color coming into their homes." They gave him an unrepairable old organ and said if he fixed it, he could have the job.

He fixed it. "They didn't know my husband very well," says Louise, Thomas's proverbial right arm, who over the years kept the company's books, answered the phones, joined the chamber of commerce, and for a time even pressed the records by hand. "I mean, this was his specialty."

After Boddie landed the job, Louise explains, he'd overhear the piano company owners telling customers on the phone, "'Now, he's a black man. But he's good and he won't bother anything or anyone.' That's kind of depressing when you hear someone say that. If he's an organ technician, he's an organ technician."

By 1959, Thomas Boddie had saved enough money to buy a house on the site of a former dairy, in a neighborhood filled with African American homeowners. He converted part of a small outbuilding into a recording studio.

"It was mainly a tape recorder there because it was still just a dirt floor," says Louise. "When we got together [in 1963], that's when we started building the rest of it." They replaced an overhead garage door with a big glass window and installed actual floors. "I learned how to pour cement and I learned how to lay tile."

About the size of a two-car garage, the studio is still pretty much intact, with the drum booth at one end and Thomas' collection of microphones pushed up against the other. Entire choirs managed to squeeze in behind the glass that separated the performers from the technician.

Thomas also designed and built a wood-burning furnace—still there—out in the studio so they could save on gas. He eventually built another such furnace in the house, too, and recycled the steam from the pressing plant through underground pipes to a generator in the house.

In the 1960s, the Boddies added the record-pressing plant. The equipment came from a Cleveland company, Kel-Mar, that had been pressing the Boddies' masters into records.

"I would go over there and they were teaching me how to operate the manual press," recalls Louise. Then the company lost some key investors and decided to close. "They said, 'Would you all like to buy the equipment?' We'll let you have it for a couple thousand dollars.'"

The Boddies managed to rustle up $2,100 to pay for two behemoth machines with manual presses. It took four minutes to press a record by hand. Louise did the manual labor, placing a ball of melted vinyl pellets into a lathe, then yanking down the heavy cover on the press. Each record took four minutes to set in the press, during which time Louise trimmed other records and put them in sleeves. Pressing an order of 1,000 records—about the maximum the Boddies could handle—took several days' work.

"It built up my arm muscles," Louise says with a laugh. "I didn't like standing on my feet that long, but I did it."

The Boddies spread plenty of mom-and-pop goodwill in Cleveland, often hosting groups from local high schools to train on their equipment. But their business took a hit after the 1966 Hough race riots in the neighborhood, says Louise. Some of the couples' white clientele flat-out told the Boddies they feared visiting their neighborhood and would no longer be coming.

But Thomas recouped the loss with increased organ business. After the Hough riots, says Louise, the white organ servicemen were afraid to work in Glenville, which was fast becoming a predominantly African-American neighborhood. "One of them said to my husband, 'Will you take over the churches that I had over there? I don't feel so safe going over there.' So Tom made a joke out of it. He said, 'If I had known that, I'd have started a riot a long time ago.'"

The record business started to decline with the introduction of cassette tapes and their DIY duplication capabilities and the oil crisis in the 1970s. But Tom and Louise had another angle: recording major church conventions around the country. They bought four hulking cassette duplication machines from a company in Indiana, lugging those in their car with a mixing board, then hiring someone on site to drag it all in on a dolly. It was a lucrative operation.

"We could produce 16 cassettes every three minutes," says Louise. They sold recordings for each convention speaker, at $7 apiece. She says the arthritic knots on her thumbs and forefingers came from taking tens of thousands of just-duplicated cassettes out of the machines.

Louise would label blank cassettes according to how many people were in attendance and how well she thought a speaker would sell. She had the names of all the speakers, and would pre-label about 50 or so for each. If a speaker sounded particularly rousing, she'd make up more cassettes on the spot.

"Usually, I was set up right outside the auditorium," she says. "So, I could here the response from the people inside. I could tell if it was quiet, 'This ain't going to be good.' But, if people were talking back to the speaker, then I thought, 'Oh, this is going to be good.'"

Louise says at first it was a little odd to have these two hipsters from Numero Group in her backyard, going through all her husbands' arcana. "We kept all of these things, but I didn't think nothing much of it. Then Dante came, and he would go, 'Oh gee, Mrs. Boddie you've got a whole history here.' He was just so excited, it made me excited.

"I hope that it will be something that people will get to know and really appreciate. Because our children—when I say our children I mean my race in particular—they need to know that you can come from nothing and become something."

—A version of this story appeared in The Root

A Cove in Collinwood

Rebecca Meiser

A*t the edge of North Collinwood,* an eastern urban neighborhood that lies on Cleveland's right hip, a row of updated 1920s-era houses look out onto the waters of Lake Erie. They are as different in style as the people who live in them—a bright yellow two-story home sits next to a spiraling white Mediterranean villa with second-floor balconies. The rumor is that some of the houses on the street were built by a shipbuilder for his daughters because he couldn't bear to have his children move away.

Collinwood started its life as a Slovenian enclave, home to polka halls, churches, and pierogi and sausage shops. In the early 1900s, its lakeside location attracted sun-seeking visitors to Euclid Beach. But as suburban flight drove the residents out, musicians and artists from Cleveland's punk underground scene moved in. "We'd go to dances and pig roasts and bowling nights," says Cindy Barber, who co-founded Beachland Ballroom, a premier indie performance stage on Waterloo Road in Collinwood. "It was cool to live here."

At the bottom stairs of one of the homes sits a converted boathouse, now called the cove, that was once thought to be used for smuggling during Prohibition. The owner of the home, Scott Stettin, repaired the cracked cement walls, polished the wood floors, and built a bar. On a recent June evening, that bar served as a resting spot for bottles of Great Lakes Brewing Company's Dortmunder Gold, baskets of barbe-

173

cue potato chips, and tall, melting candles. Christmas lights loop along the cove's gray walls, a neon blue Pabst sign blinks on and off like a traffic light. A small makeshift stage, covered in gray carpet, sits at the rear of the cove. Stettin, who owns an upscale hair salon in North Olmsted, says he and friends constructed the stage as a means of "leveling out the room." His wife, Meredith Pangrace, disagrees. "You guys built the stage because you wanted to be on stage."

Most Sunday nights, a small group of thirty and forty-something male friends gather to jam. Officially, they call themselves The Cove Men. Unofficially, they refer to themselves as "local idiots who think they're great."

The group is made up of artists, former accountants, and business owners—most of whom have not had formal musical training. Chris Kennedy, who started these sessions about five years ago, bought a guitar for the first time when he entered the Peace Corps in 2000. "I thought I would learn how to play in Micronesia, but it turns out [the residents there] played entirely different tempos and keys," he says. He learned about two chords, and got his friend Frank Revy to start playing guitar with him when he returned. Revy agreed because "it made our drinking more constructive," he says.

But not everyone is a novice. Sean Seibert played the tuba in college. In his high school yearbook from 1989, he wrote that his future plans were to "eat pizza six nights a week, play in the Ohio State marching band, and dot the i" [in the Ohio script spelled out at halftime]. Seibert accomplished both. His senior year, when Ohio State played Michigan, he "cried twice," he says. "Once, before the game, when I learned I would be the I dotter, and then after the game, when we got whipped."

As the lake outside the cove's door flows, the crew picks up their instruments. Seibert takes a seat behind the keyboard, Kennedy settles himself onto a stool with his guitar, and Stettin picks up a pair of drumsticks. They play William DeVaughn's "Be Thankful for What You Got." Sean's shaggy blond head is bent down in concentration, Stettin pounds on the drum open-fisted, and Revy hits a xylophone, fastened to the wall. But after a few notes, they fade out, each eventually putting down their instruments.

"I'm not really sure how to end that one," Stettin admits.

They decide to play "Springtime in Cleveland" instead. The song sounds similar to their other three songs, "Summertime in Cleveland,"

"Wintertime in Cleveland," and "Fall in Cleveland," all composed by Stettin on bar napkins.

Here's how it goes: "I love the springtime in Cleveland / We kick the snow around/ohhh we like to party down . . . in Cleveland." "'Wintertime in Cleveland' is a little less upbeat," Stettin admits.

Stettin uses his drum sticks as a conductor's baton. Revy shakes his shaved head, and Kennedy, having placed his beer on the head of a bongo, sings into the microphone. Pangrace strums along with a mandolin.

Outside, summertime in Cleveland is pushing through the clouds. Jackson, the dog is barking. There is no one on the beach—really, there is no beach, anyway—but the cymbals ripple through the waves and the Miller Lite empties are carefully stacked to make sure they don't fall into the lake, outside the cove.

Yes, Hardcore

Chris Wise

Things will be different then;
the sun will rise from here.
　　　　　　—The Dead Boys

W*hen I was a teenager, my friends and I* would drive up to Cleveland at night for punk shows at Peabody's, the Euclid Tavern, and the Agora. Rounding that last bend on I-77 past 490, we were always awed by the skyline coming into view, foregrounded by LTV Steel's towering flare-stack blasting its flame into sky. We also amused ourselves with the possible meaning of the area road signs with "HC" in the middle of a circle and a big red slash through it.

Cleveland's out of hot chocolate? No helicopter commuting? Hairless camels prohibited?! Or the worst possible explanation: *No hardcore.*

We were big fans of hardcore music—bands in the tradition of Black Flag, Bad Brains, Minor Threat—and aspired to the scene's rough and gritty DIY ethic. We loved rummaging through the bins at Chris' Warped Records, loved letting bands like Ascension, Integrity, and Choice kick our asses. To us, with its fire and darkness, pub piss and punk rock, Cleveland epitomized all that was hardcore. "No hardcore? What gives, Cleveland?" we'd joke.

Of course, Cleveland is hardcore. Throughout its history, the city has abided in flame and ash, oil and steel, thriving and suffering at the collision point between nature and industry, man and machine in a perpetual mosh pit of reckless abandon. Its landscapes have been polluted and neglected, and the people who still call the city home have been hardened by years of economic decline and cultural indignity.

To cope, the city has tried to turn perceived weaknesses into strengths with catchy slogans like *Cleveland: You've Got to Be Tough* or *Visit Cleveland. We'll Keep the River on for You.* Its people have had to carry around punk-rock attitudes, in case they might need to unleash them on those who try to put their city down.

You don't love the Browns? Fuck You!
(Paraphrased from the message on a hat my dad used to wear.)

Unfortunately, nothing epitomizes the abuse Cleveland has taken more than the Cuyahoga River catching on fire, not just once in 1969, but more than six times since 1868. A couple of those fires set the whole Flats district ablaze, destroying businesses and bridges, almost taking down the whole city. It's still the critics' favorite jab and our favorite hardcore emblem of pride.

I used to swim in the Cuyahoga as a kid, used to joyfully collect turtles and tadpoles in the summer sun. Generations have been baptized in the river of fire. It's nothing to be proud of, but surviving despite such an environment is.

In the punk scene, a person who only dresses the part but puts no effort into really supporting or contributing to the scene is called a poser (or arrogant asshole). In an underdog place like Cleveland, it's nice to believe that at least we're not posers, that we have a special propensity for the authentic.

But authenticity can only feel legit when it comes from being honest and committed to what you do and believe. True to the city's hardcore spirit, Clevelanders have banded together to bring our river and its surrounding natural beauty back from the dead.

Work to preserve the Ohio and Erie Canal has helped Cleveland parks again live up to their "Emerald Necklace" nickname. The towpath trail along the canalway is near completion of its 100-mile course from New Philadelphia (south of Canton) northward along the Cuyahoga to the shores of Lake Erie, cutting through the city's industrial core on way to its northern terminus.

The reclamation of land for the ten-foot-wide trail has been a painfully challenging and costly enterprise. Braving ahead in true DIY fashion, however, advocates have forged trail openings in Cuyahoga Heights alongside rolling industrial railcars and transformed a vacant concrete lot into the Cuyahoga Rowing Foundation at Rivergate Park.

Ecological renewal is happening. And rusted train cars, crumbling canal locks, and ruined bridges *will* be left along the trails in the parks as stand-in memorials to the past (no commemorative plaques really required). This is something to truly be proud of.

Karma has been a bitch, but we're tough enough to push onward. It's the only way. That is why we are enthusiastically filling neglected parks with flowers, running for city council, staying local to start businesses. That is why some of us sign up for the Burning River 100, a 100-mile ultra-marathon that spans the length of the entire Cuyahoga Valley, incorporating many of its parks' trails, from Squire's Castle in Willoughby Hills to downtown Cuyahoga Falls. We are hoping the river and land of ours might begin to forgive us, get back on good terms with our town again.

The "mistake by the lake" label has long been our inherited sin, but hopefully it's a *felix culpa*, and working our redemption will prove sweet.

Remembering Mr. Stress, Live at the Euclid Tavern

Philip Turner

G*rowing up in the hotbed of rock n' roll* that was Cleveland in the '60s and '70s, I began going out to hear live music even before I had turned 16. Music Hall with its fixed rows of seats trimmed in maroon velvet was a regular venue for bills such as Cream with Canned Heat; the Grateful Dead with the New Riders of the Purple Sage; Traffic; John Mayall; the Allman Brothers; and The Band, among many other acts. In 1972, just after turning eighteen, then Ohio's legal drinking age, I discovered a live music venue that was even more fun as a hang-out than Music Hall.

On the eastern edge of University Circle, at the corner of Euclid Avenue and 116th Street, sat the Euclid Tavern, where the venerable Cleveland bluesman Mr. Stress and his four-piece band joined forces every Wednesday and Saturday night for a long-running residency. Mr. Stress was the Paul Butterfield of Cleveland—a white bluesman who sang and played harmonica and led his band with an unerring sense of what made the blues entertaining and sustaining for live music lovers. He was always comfortable on stage with a cohort of diverse sidemen, young and old, black and white, tattooed players and professorial pianists. The club included a central music room with a low stage for the band and a dance floor, an outdoor area in back, plus a basement bar. It was a veritable cruise ship of nightlife. During breaks between sets I often made new friends in my ambles around the lively deck.

In the room opposite the stage was the main bar, a long hitching post of a drinks station where multiple bartenders pulled beer taps and poured liquor. Behind and above them was a sign that became a watchword in my life: "It's hard to soar like an eagle when you're on the ground with the turkeys."

Mr. Stress—real name Bill Miller—was a TV repairman by day. "Stress," as most people called him, was a big reader, a history buff who avidly consumed books, including many on the Vietnam War. In 1978, when my family and I began running Undercover Books, a bookstore in Shaker Heights, I'd order Nam books that Stress asked me about and bring them to the club for him. (Sometimes he paid for them, sometimes I just gave them to him—my personal payback to Stress for the generous enrichment he always lent to the Cleveland music scene.)

Like me, many Stress fans came to the Euclid Tavern every week. I was friendly with Danny Palumbo, who got around in a wheelchair. Danny worked for the State of Ohio in workplace compliance for accommodating the disabled. Never hindered in his enjoyment of the fine blues that Mr. Stress and the band played, Danny would dance in his chair along with everyone else crowding the wooden dance floor, boogieing to up-tempo numbers like "Crosscut Saw" and "Firing Line," or swaying to laments such as the mournful "Black Night." Danny had a colorful way of talking about the female friends he'd meet each week at the bar, and I recall him once saying of a certain Tanya, a particularly cute and curvaceous regular, that given the chance he'd eagerly "drink her bathwater."

Stress enjoyed bantering with his bandmates and regulars got to know his repertoire very well. As Stress would reach the punch line to one of his hoary gags, a bartender would chime the tip bell, a baddaboom underlining the corny humor. The exterior of the building that housed the Euclid Tavern was a dark reddish-brown brick, as weathered as the nearby streets. Stress dubbed it "the sick brick," a rueful yet fond homage to the innumerable nights of alcoholic excess that had been committed within its walls.

Sometime in the early '80s, Stress put out an album, *Mr. Stress Live at the Euclid Tavern*. I still treasure the vinyl LP, and listened to it while composing these recollections. After moving to New York City in 1985, I would sometimes return to the club when visiting family back home. Except for Stress, I never saw the old crew. As years passed, I occasionally wondered whether he was still playing at the Euclid Tavern, and playing in Cleveland at all. I also wondered if the Euclid Tavern was still standing at 116th Street, even as the rest of University Circle underwent many makeovers and Cleveland picked itself up off the mat of urban decline time and again. My sister Pamela Turner still lives in Cleveland, and she found the "sick brick" for me, taking a photo I've posted on my website. I phoned the establishment and asked a bartender who answered if Mr. Stress still plays there. Sounding a bit surprised, he replied, "No, he hasn't played here for a couple years."

I later spoke with *Plain Dealer* reporter John Petkovic, who'd written a 2011 story about Stress that reported that in 1993 he'd had a heart attack. Stress also told Petkovic, "I woke up one morning and . . . I had lost a third of my vision. I've heard it comes from blowing so hard, you pop blood vessels. I can't drive or get around as well. But it ain't stopping me from playing the blues."

Petkovic referred me to Alan Greene, a Cleveland musician who played gigs with Stress as late as 2010. Alan said Stress now considers himself in "semi-retirement." Alan also mentioned that next New Year's Eve, Stress will turn 70, which brought back a flood of rich memories from great New Year's Eve shows when Stress and revelers raucously marked a new year and Bill's birthday. Alan also mentioned that when Stress was born a minute after midnight in 1943, he was feted as Cleveland's firstborn of the new year—an auspicious beginning for what turned out to be a great life and career.

I will always fondly recall the many nights of fine blues and camaraderie I enjoyed thanks to Mr. Stress and his talented bandmates. Now living in New York City, I remain a devotee of going out to hear live music, a happy habit I began forty years ago at the Euclid Tavern, listening to Mr. Stress.

Jane Scott's Rust Belt Values

Elizabeth Weinstein

"All of us who have lived here in Cleveland have Jane (Scott) stories."

I t's July 5, 2012—a year and one day after the death of Jane Scott, Cleveland's legendary rock journalist, at age 92—and Rock & Roll Hall of Fame & Museum president and CEO Terry Stewart is addressing a crowd of about 50 friends, fans, and reporters who have gathered in the Rock Hall's lower lobby to honor her memory.

Stewart is right. Mention "Jane Scott" to someone you've just met at a local bar, for instance, and they will most likely flash a genuine smile, put a hand to their heart, and wax nostalgic about that one time 30 years ago when they sat next to the pioneering reporter at a show at the Agora, and how the first question out of her mouth was, "Where do you go to high school?" Or they will tell you how fearless she was—charging into mosh pits at the ripe age of 80 and traipsing past threatening security guards to gain backstage access at concerts. A perfect blend of Rust Belt values, Scott was soft-spoken and humble, passionate about rock and roll, and unflinchingly determined to be the best in her field. She never took no for an answer, spent many late nights slumped over her typewriter in the newsroom, and was not intimidated by anyone—not even the most foul-mouthed of rock bands. Jane Scott loved Cleveland, and Cleveland loved Jane Scott.

Behind Stewart is a life-size bronze sculpture of Scott, which is hidden, for now, under a giant piece of dark cloth. The sculpture, by

Cleveland artist David Deming, is a gift to the Rock Hall from Scott's surviving nieces Linda Cook and Sally Gooding and nephew Bill Scott, all of whom are present for the event.

"(Jane) was considered to be . . . the first and one of the most significant rock journalists of all time," Stewart tells the crowd. "She covered (musicians) small, large, insignificant, emerging—every artist that passed through this town." And Scott, he notes, was very influential in bringing the Rock Hall to Cleveland in 1995. He then calls up to the podium Cleveland rocker Michael Stanley (a longtime friend of Jane Scott's), Scott's nieces and nephew, and sculptor Deming to unveil what is under the cloth. Gasps, applause, and the flashing of a dozen news cameras follow, as everyone moves closer to marvel at Scott's likeness.

Yep. That's her, all right. She's seated, ankles crossed, on a bench, with a ticket stub pinned to her shirt. She's wearing her signature pageboy haircut and large red glasses, and her overstuffed purse contains a jar of peanut butter (Scott always packed a peanut butter sandwich for her rock reporting adventures; it was the only food that never spoiled at those long outdoor concerts). In her hands is a reporter's notebook with her two favorite interview questions scribbled on a sheet of paper: "What is your favorite color?" and "Where did you go to high school?"

Later, in the administrative offices of the Rock Hall, Scott's niece Sally Gooding gushes about the sculpture: "She aged so much at the end of her life, but when I was sitting next to (the sculpture), it was like the Aunt Jane I really remember."

That Aunt Jane was Cleveland's foremost authority on all things rock and roll for more than 50 years. A Girl Scout and model student, Scott, who was born on May 3, 1919, made it her mission to treat all people—even rock stars—alike and with kindness. She graduated from Lakewood High School in 1937 and from the University of Michigan in 1941, where she majored in English and drama. Following college graduation. Scott enlisted in WAVES (Women Accepted for Volunteer Emergency Service), the women's branch of the United States Navy, and rose to the rank of Lieutenant. Then, on March 24, 1952, Scott was hired by the *Plain Dealer*, one of Cleveland's daily newspapers. Coincidentally, that was just three days after Alan Freed's Moondog Coronation Ball at the old Cleveland Arena. Freed's event went down in history as the world's first rock music concert.

Scott worked for the *Cleveland Plain Dealer* from 1952 to 2002, and is credited with being the first rock journalist at a major daily US newspaper. Remarkably, she was a woman who thrived in an area of journalism that has long been saturated with mostly young male reporters. First hired as a society assistant, covering the goings-on of Cleveland's social elite, she was given a "little blue book" that contained the names and telephone numbers of everyone her editors deemed "important" enough to cover. Scott soon moved onto writing and editing simultaneously for the paper's "Senior Class" section, which was targeted at senior citizens, and the "Teen Page," which was aimed at Cleveland's young people.

Everything changed on September 15, 1964, when Scott attended an electrifying concert by four young British men—John Lennon, Paul McCartney, Ringo Starr, and George Harrison—at Cleveland's Public Hall. She attended the Beatles concert because the kids who read her "Teen Page" were buzzing about it, and she wanted to see what all the fuss was about.

"I never before saw thousands of 14-year-old girls all screaming and yelling," Scott later years told the *Plain Dealer*'s current pop music critic, John Soeder. "I realized this was a phenomenon . . . . The whole world changed."

Two years later, on August 14, 1966, Scott was sent to the old Hotel Cleveland Sheraton to attend a Beatles press conference. The band was in town for a concert that evening and Scott was determined to interview them. Once inside, then forty-something Scott made a beeline for then twenty-something Paul McCartney, but so did all of the other reporters—mostly male television reporters who obstructed her view with their bulky microphones and video cameras. So instead, she approached Lennon to talk. She asked him, "How's it going?" He told her, "Well, it's not as good as it was. Who said it's going to last forever?" She wrote that down, and smiled at the irony decades later. The Beatles, of course, became a pop culture institution—and so did Jane Scott.

After Beatlemania, Scott's "Teen Page" gradually morphed from a listing of teen dances and sporting events into a rock and roll music page, and music took over Scott's life and career. She attended about 10,000 concerts over her lifetime, and landed interviews with every major musician who came through Cleveland, including the Rolling Stones, Led Zeppelin, Jim Morrison, David Bowie, Janis Joplin, Aretha Franklin, the Beastie Boys, Bruce Springsteen, Lyle Lovett, and many more.

Scott had a habit of incorporating everyone around her into her articles, and, unlike many rock journalists past and present, she treated teenage fans with respect, quoting them in her articles and turning to them to help her predict who would become rock's biggest stars. People loved and respected Scott in large part because she approached writing about music objectively and enthusiastically, and always kept an open mind. With a genuine and warm demeanor, and an infectious laugh, she easily endeared herself to rappers, heavy metal rockers, pop stars, and readers alike. Her passion for music was limitless—and contagious.

In addition to being one of the first rock reporters for a daily newspaper, Scott also became the oldest living rock journalist, working steadily until her retirement at age 82, in 2002. In a field notorious for its high burnout rate (due to frequent late nights, eardrum-shattering bands, and the fast pace of the rock and roll lifestyle), Scott outlasted most of her peers. Writing about music was such a big part of Scott's life that even after retiring, she still attended concerts and took copious notes wherever she went—filing them away for a memoir she never got around to writing.

Despite several proposals from suitors, Scott never married. At 80, she found love with a man named Jim Smith, and he passed away six years later, in October 2004.

Her first true love was rock and roll. When Scott passed away on July 4, 2011, at age 92, hundreds of articles about her life—and her importance in rock and roll history—appeared in newsprint and online. And, on August 28, 2011, nearly 900 people crowded into the Rock Hall for a music-filled memorial service in her honor.

The last years of Scott's life were marked by dementia, but the memories she created through her articles will always live on in Cleveland, and in rock journalism history. Her statue will remain permanently in the lower lobby of the Rock Hall, and Scott's family has generously donated an extensive collection of materials (including about 4,000 LPs, autographs from all four Beatles, historical photographs, and more than 300 of her writing-filled notebooks) from her estate to the Rock Hall's Library and Archives at Cuyahoga Community College.

"She never threw anything away," says Scott's niece, Linda Cook, with a laugh.

Thank goodness for that.

VII. Culture

Bob Perkowski

A (Really Nice) Drink for the Working Man

Alissa Nutting

The proclamation that I was moving to Cleveland last summer aroused powerful reactions of sympathy in others. My friends made facial expressions befitting news of an inoperable brain tumor or a nuclear-plant meltdown. In retrospect, I'm surprised no one showed up at my door with a casserole. When I was explaining my choice to one acquaintance—how I was moving for work and benefits, etc.—he stopped me mid-sentence: "Getting healthcare isn't much of a perk if you're moving to a place where life isn't worth living." He said this with the slow frustration of someone forced to explain a concept that should be very obvious, like why a five-year-old can't get a driver's license..

I've lived in Cleveland for over a year now, and I'm pretty sure that if my friend could sample the various growlers of craft beer in my refrigerator, he would be willing to eat crow just for the chance to wash it down with more and more delicious Ohio microbrew.

As a newcomer to the Rust Belt, I have been delightedly astonished by the amazing food and beer to be enjoyed. I have gone up several pant sizes. I have, since moving to Cleveland, increased my featherweight drinking tolerance (the unfortunate genetic distillation of several generations of temperance-embracing ancestors) to a still unrespectable but personal-best division of lightweight. The microbreweries and gastropubs in Cleveland are so good. To me, their design and décor is a perfect example of Rust Belt Chic.

"Chic" anything (shabby chic, boho chic) seems to be a juxtaposed type of gentrification, a blend of upper-class elements with lower-class ones. In these Rust Belt Chic bars and restaurants, traditional industrial and rugged interiors—exposed water lines, walls of reclaimed wood—are blended with upscale food and drink. The result is beer and food that would please discriminating palates in an atmosphere that doesn't feel intimidating. The integration of blue-collar accessories (monochromatic, unbleached industrial paper towels on holders of rusted pipe in lieu of napkins, for example) and union-friendly Marxist service practices (many do not accept reservations) combined with $20 cheeseburgers speaks towards an aesthetic that purposefully shirks glitz and glamour. These establishments feel like a brother-done-good in a large family of working-class watering holes: These are bars that went off to college but returned to their hometown to give back some of the worldliness they gained. They didn't forget where they came from, and they don't want to make the kids who knew them back when uncomfortable.

They also don't want to be called sissies. As a woman, I'm fully aware of the ways it's the Rust Belt and not the Garter Belt. These places are dripping with stereotypical masculinity. There's not a drop of pink. Nothing shines or shimmers; anything metallic is brushed or matte instead of sparkling chrome. If you're not having beer, you're encouraged to go with whiskey or bourbon. I love whiskey but I haven't yet begun sailing its extensive waters in the bars here, because there are just too many beers to try first—kind of like how you could only listen to music made in the '70s for your entire life and still not uncover all the good stuff that's out there. When I once ordered a chocolate martini for a friend in a Rust Belt Chic restaurant, I found myself whispering; the phrase "chocolate martini" had a contraband feel. There was a small discussion of whether or not it could even be done (Me: "Is that possible?" My waitress: "Let me see." To her boss: "Can we do a chocolate martini?" Her boss, after some pause: "We can do that."). But it certainly wasn't on the menu.

Coming from Vegas, a place where the point of wealth is to flaunt it, one of the most interesting aspects of the Rust Belt Chic aesthetic is its preoccupation with disguising prosperity. This rough, unfinished design speaks to a sensibility that claims external packaging is neither important nor indicative of the quality to be found within—or perhaps the insider statement that the outside can purposefully serve as camouflage. Not unlike the female peacock, Rust Belt Chic bars and restaurants use plain design as protection; the highbrow features of these venues that might seem out-of-place in the Rust Belt are safely hidden inside the menus. This also gives locals a sense of having insider knowledge that these drinking holes are swanker than the average passerby might guess.

While a lot of work no doubt goes into the purposefully "unfinished" aesthetic, this kind of décor does produce a sense that distractions aren't welcome and a focal shift onto the drinks and conversation. It's not a scenic setting. In fact it feels like a place you've come to temporarily take shelter, and there's something metaphorically nice about that, particularly in the winter. It's a bit dreamlike: You enter a room whose features have a lot in common with a long-deserted barn, and suddenly, thankfully, you're drinking the best IPA you've ever had in your life. It's the perfect end to a hard day's work, but this is where the socioeconomic class distinction found in "chic" comes in. Although workers with collars of all colors could enjoy the fare at these establishments, only the upper crust could afford to eat and drink at Rust Belt Chic microbreweries after every working day.

How We Arrived At Braised Beef Cheek Pierogis

Douglas Trattner

*I*n hindsight it's fitting that my very first restaurant review—over a decade ago—involved a modest corned beef joint. Though the Cleveland dining scene slowly was gaining speed, that mile-high corned beef sandwich proved the ideal bookend for the journey to come.

Just weeks after starting as the *Free Times* restaurant critic, I was tasked with compiling one of those dreaded "Top 50" lists. Turned out, it was more difficult to draft than an inoffensive best man speech. To populate the list I was compelled to include dusty chestnuts on life support, dreadfully dull temples of fine dining, and life-threatening ethnic dives. Worse, I was reduced to expanding Cleveland's borders clear out to Akron, Hudson and Cuyahoga Falls.

Cut to 2011 when I was asked by my editors at *Scene* to compile a similar list of top Cleveland eateries. The assignment proved exponentially more difficult this time around—but for the opposite reason. In ten years' time the Cleveland restaurant scene had exploded, making the project more an exercise in editing than addition. Great restaurants would be left out. Chefs would be offended. Diners would scream bloody murder that their favorite bistro was criminally excluded from the list.

The Cleveland dining scene officially had arrived.

I'm frequently asked why the Cleveland food scene is far and away more progressive than those of similarly sized cities. While there's no single answer, one of the biggest reasons is that Cleveland is home.

Invariably, young chefs leave their nests to study, work, and explore diverse kitchens around the globe. The difference is that Cleveland-born chefs boomerang back.

Michael Symon. Dante Boccuzzi. Jonathon Sawyer. Zack Bruell. Doug Katz. Karen Small. Rocco Whalen. Sergio Abramof. Brandt Evans. I've spoken to these chefs and many like them. I asked them "why Cleveland?" as opposed to starlet cuisine scenes like Chicago or New York. Yes, it is home, but so what? That is, what gives Cleveland a magnetism that draws the native culinary son back?

While everybody has his or her own reasons, many I've spoken to claim family, friends, and quality of life as primary motivations. And when those chefs do return they discover a culturally rich community boasting a verdant farmers market system, venerable West Side Market, colleagues uncharacteristically supportive of one another, and a bona fide regional cuisine borne from the home kitchens of countless nimble-fingered immigrants.

As well, Cleveland is a real city subsisting on real food with real roots. Cleveland chefs—good chefs, brave chefs—look both backward and forward when cultivating a cuisine. Symon famously elevated the humble pierogi by swapping the lowly potato filling for succulent braised beef cheeks, the perfect marriage of ethnic food and current nose-to-tail trends.

But without fearless, trusting and enthusiastic diners, even the most talented chef is stymied. Cleveland diners, for the large part, have kept pace with the progress. How else could a chef get away with selling a whole roasted pig face—as Sawyer does at Greenhouse Tavern—or *pied de cochon* (pig's feet)—as Bruell does at L'Albatros? Ambitious dining has become sport in Cleveland, buoyed by a fervent social media community that seems to have a boundless appetite for culinary adventure.

But like the chefs who cook with one foot in the past and the other in the present, local diners have not turned their bellies away from tradition. The two most popular eateries in Cleveland, I would wager, are Lola and Slyman's Deli. At 90 years old, Sokolowski's University Inn is an absolute relic among newborns—but its unassuming Eastern European food also is one of the biggest draws in town.

If there is a common thread among our favorite restaurants—be they highbrow or low, serving braised beef or corned—it's that they are authentic. If we Clevelanders are good at anything, it's spotting a phony from a mile away. We support local businesses run by people—born here or adopted—who stay true to their mission. Chains, while certainly present, increasingly get the cold shoulder in the 216.

When it comes to the food scene, Cleveland will never be New York, Chicago or San Francisco. But then again, who the hell wants it to be?

Lessons of Industrial Tourism

Mark Tebeau

L *ike other folks living in placeless and rootless mass-produced suburbs,* Clevelanders have been busy rediscovering their heritage through the
city's industrial legacy—exploring the ruins of plants long abandoned
or touring sextant manufacturing facilities. In 2011, for example, Rose
Iron Works, arguably the oldest operating facility of its kind in the United States, hosted sold-out tours of its historic facility, located along
Superior Avenue. Visitors to the bowels of the 100-year old shop encounter the tools, the elegant repoussé, and "catalog" of decorative
ironwork scavenged from Europe in the wake of World War I.

Some cultural critics have deemed such industrial tourism, and
the photographs that often accompany it, as "ruin porn." They suggest
that such activities transform our industrial history into another com-
modity in a consumer society. And, these critics note, civic boosters
use industrial tourism nostalgically to help drum up public support for
sometimes questionable economic and urban development initiatives.
Perhaps. But Rose Iron Works surely tells a more complex story, especially when we consider the art inside the factory.

Nestled in the rafters of Rose Iron Works is a detailed frieze, over
50 feet long, that depicts the history of ironwork. Stunning in its details,
display of expert craftsmanship, and enormous scale, this singular work
of art embodies the history of ironworking as well as the history of our
city. Crafted by Martin Rose, Paul Feher, and the shop's workers during

the 1930s, this singular frieze was Rose's clever way to keep his workers busy during a rough economic stretch. (Sound familiar?)

Rose created this visual history of craftsmanship based on apprenticeships at various iron works in Budapest in the 1890s and through more formal training and courses he took in Vienna, where he studied under urban planner Camillo Sitte. Influential among designers and planners in the late 19th and early 20th centuries, Sitte argued for an urban design based in artistry, not efficiency. He advocated for irregular and artistic spaces, shaped by both greenery and ornament, and built with the highest quality of craftsmanship. In his often-cited 1889 manifesto, *The Art of Building Cities*, Sitte confronted the challenges of building modern cities by drawing upon historical examples to rethink how planners could build cities on a human scale, with well-conceived public spaces.

Sitte's teaching about design, and in particular a lecture he delivered on the history of the craft, made quite an impression on the young apprentice Martin Rose, who would join millions of Central Europeans and emigrate to the United States.

At the turn of the 20th Century, Rose abandoned the rigid political, economic, and social structures of the Austro-Hungarian Empire, and brought his arts and craft training to Cleveland. Once here, he took commissions for some of the city's most notable buildings and worked with the region's leading architects and designers. His firm, Rose Iron Works, would craft the decorative metalwork inside and outside downtown office buildings and department stores and build ornamentation for elaborately constructed residences along Euclid Avenue. The firm even forged the futuristic aluminum zodiac artwork developed by Viktor Schreckengost that graced the entrance to Cleveland Hopkins Airport for many years. Ironically, even as Rose shaped the city's landscape and succeeded financially, the ethos of industrialism and modernity undercut the aesthetic ethos of wrought-iron craftsmanship. Increasingly, builders wanted mass production and efficiency, not beauty.

Rather than shrink in the face of these demands, Rose coupled ornamental iron work with the sensibility of Art Deco, producing work that brought the firm its greatest renown: a fireplace screen that uses wrought iron to imagine the streamlined design of modernity, presently on display at the Cleveland Museum of Art. At the same time, Rose and Feher produced the remarkable frieze that sits in the rafters of the shop. In so doing, they playfully captured Camillo Sitte's critique of industrial efficiency as a design principle, celebrating the history of ironwork and the power of beauty, art, and craft to transform our lives.

Touring Rose Iron Works does more than conjure wistful memories of Cleveland's industrial past, just as the frieze in the firm's rafters gives more than a simple history lesson. It provides a window into how a previous artists, innovators, and designers confronted the dislocations of industrial change. In reimagining Sitte's history of iron working in wrought iron, Rose fused past and present into an iconic work of art that embodied Sitte's approach to art, design, and cities.

If we cannot escape the idioms of the past, we surely should not allow ourselves to be tyrannized by nostalgia either. Just as it was for Martin Rose and his teacher Camillo Sitte, the past is but a tool to help us reimagine and reinvent the future. We should follow their lead and forge new and distinctive places that transcend the clichés of deindustrialization, and build communities on an artistic and human-scale vision for our lives and landscapes—including right here in Cleveland.

Randall Tiedman: Genius Loci

Douglas Max Utter

Editors' Note: Randall Tiedman died on November 4, 2012. This second edition of Rust Belt Chic *is dedicated to his memory.*

T*he far edge of Cleveland's Tremont district* drops off abruptly, affording a sudden wide-angle view of industry and commerce in the valley below. A traffic circle at that spot swirls cars onto Interstate 71, or alternatively shunts them down Quigley Road toward the big box stores at Steelyard Commons, against a backdrop of intertwining highway pylons and bridges. To the west, buildings and properties owned by the global steel and mining company ArcelorMittal spread along the banks of the Cuyahoga, and everywhere exploitation, consumption, and profit commingle in amoral layers. Bearing the deep imprint of human ambition and need, the area is like an economic Olduvai Gorge—or maybe a slope in Purgatory, arguably minus the spiritual learning curve..

Such terrain can also be mined and exploited by the imagination. Northern Ohio artist Randall Tiedman does just that. Until 2005 he painted tensely expressive, tactile visions most often focused on the human body, but since then he has rendered an oddly wider world. His method has been to salvage peripheral impressions of industrial views, restored from the margins of perception to form the breaking lines of gray and umber mindscapes. These vistas don't seem invented, but in some sense recovered or even revealed. Tiedman's large (typically about 4" × 3") acrylic paintings present fraught re-visions of contemporary wastelands, glimpsed from above in a sulfurous near darkness. They are the stuff of epic poetry, an account of the wreckage that attends great sin. If you squint across the aforementioned Industrial Valley (really its name, according to Google) at dusk, you glimpse the sort of end-times panorama that Tiedman improvises in paintings.

Tiedman's highly unusual romantic-apocalyptic slant is exciting to contemporary curators and collectors. He is adding to the repertoire of regionalism; clearly this is a far cry from your grandparents' painted midwestern reveries.

Tiedman's new fans include national art magazines, as well as major museums and collections. Twice featured in the high-profile publication *New American Painting*, he has also recently been collected by the Albright Knox Museum in Buffalo, the Butler Museum of American Art in Youngstown, the Erie Art Museum, and several corporate collections, most notably Progressive Insurance. At the further end of a career marked by solitary, almost monkish activity, these events are practically a firestorm. And presumably they're just beginning.

Barely within Cleveland's city limits, a few miles out from downtown in North Collinwood, Randall Tiedman has lived most of his life in an up-down style duplex purchased by his grandparents in the early years of the last century. His older brother Richard (who writes commentary and criticism about classical music) occupies the downstairs suite. Grovewood Avenue, which is part of one of the east side's main bus routes, bumps along a few feet past a narrow strip of front yard, and the neighbors' houses squeeze in from adjoining lots. About a block to the west, a grassy athletic field spreads across a dozen acres and a small abandoned community pool yawns nearby. Dating from the 1960s, the scene seems like a city planner's meditation on absence and changing times. But the location seems to have stubbornly good karma; a well-appointed new Collinwood Recreation Center recently opened on the other side of the road, at one end of an otherwise decaying shopping complex. Whether the zeitgeist is coming or going, the restless shifting of priorities and populations continues, channeled through the hard decades.

All of this finds its way into Tiedman's never-lands, though it's hard to say just how. He improvises without preliminary sketches or photo references in a tiny back bedroom studio, hunkered in front of oversized etching-weight sheets of paper, grafting hypostatic spiritual scenery from back brain to painted surface as if by sorcery or prayer. Fragments of the fences and batting cages, benches and bleachers on Grovewood show up in the pictures, but so does everything else; Tiedman finds grist in every corner of his reality. A short walk from his house to a bridge over the CSX rail yards reveals enough industrial strength creative DNA to power a whole fleet of his paintings. Along the way the road seems pregnant with a life of its own, finally buckling and splitting apart at the corner of a short street named "Darwin." From this point you can peer through a fence and see the lumbering freight cars. Punctuated by a gothic-looking grain elevator to the north and the white vanes of a wind turbine to the south, intertwining tracks flex like exposed back muscles, pushing the residential zones of North Collinwood away from the derelict GM and GE factories to the south.

And if, like Tiedman in his paintings, you levitate above this scene and withdraw to a greater height, it becomes clear that the most important view by far, from Collinwood or anywhere else in northern Ohio, is Lake Erie, which shears off all other structures and doings like a titanic guillotine. You may forget that they're there, yet no more than five blocks from the Grovewood house the gray waters loom almost secretly, out of all proportion to daily life, as improbable as Leviathan. Mostly hidden from view either by buildings or the lay of the land, the lake is the priceless dreamtime of the city, cradling actual and imaginary worlds in the same primordial gesture, never to be landlocked or subdivided. Its presence in Tiedman's paintings is perhaps the crucial way in which he tells the secret truth of place, a secret which his images so compellingly argue. We realize that the fundament of Tiedman's tragically peaking and crashing visions isn't earth at all, but water. Paintings like *St. Neot's Margin* (2008) or *Night's Speechless Carnival* (2010) have sometimes been tagged post-apocalyptic, but a close look hints at sources in the Book of Genesis rather than the Book of Revelation. These are places half-drowned and overturned by a great flood.

The scale and corrosive grandeur of the mess in and around America's cities surely does suggest a once and future kingdom of titanic, chthonic powers—especially if you gaze by moonlight, or by the glare of sodium compression streetlights, as Tiedman seems to do. Bearing titles with classical or biblical resonance, like the *Limbus Patrum* and *Promethean Web* series, these paintings evoke a psychological reality correlative to everyday experience, emptied of persons but filled with surmise—observed not from any modern roadway but, despite their references to up-to-date-looking stadiums and specifically industrial structures like water treatment facilities, tremblingly, as if at the reins of a chariot. This is our world seen through the eyes of angel, or demon.

It's no wonder these vertiginous works have earned Tiedman an enthusiastic new audience over the past half decade. His earlier styles (his first paintings date from the late 1960s) applied some of the same qualities to renderings of the human figure. But these newer, hallucinatory hills, doom-colored tarns, and the hurricane-like devastation swirling around them convey a very different immediacy and conviction. Perhaps they strike iPad-weary eyes as nearly classical, while retaining a cinematic sweep that feels freshly scripted, as if urgently dictated by subconscious impulses. Tiedman explores as he prophesies, digging among the roots of fascination, evoking the seductions of disaster, distance, and power.

Tiedman is a slightly stooped but still imposingly tall man in his early sixties. Despite the neutralizing effects of age and a neatly trimmed gray beard, he retains the intensity of a natural athlete. It makes sense that among the complex roots of Tiedman's self-taught practice, Abstract Expressionism stands out as a central inspiration—a school of painting much inflected by existentialist thought, emphasizing above all gesture and presence and the native spontaneity of truth-telling. Of all the loosely knit groups that invented postwar modernity, the New York–based Abstract Expressionists were the most triumphantly individualistic, and athletic in that they competed in life-long agons not only with each other, but with themselves.

Tiedman is cut from that cloth.

He began to draw and paint when he was a teenager, interests strengthened by visits to the Cleveland Museum of Art and by his friendship at that time with Gary Dumm, the future cartoonist of *American Splendor* fame. He drew soldiers and their girlfriends when he was drafted, and made collages when he came close to dying, not in a firefight but in boot camp during a deadly outbreak of spinal meningitis. Following eleven months of service in Danang, news of his mother's death arrived and the army sent him home. A series of jobs followed, including one with Dumm at Kaye's Books in downtown Cleveland. Eventually he set tled into a job as clerk at the Cleveland Public Library, preparing books and materials for the blind. That turned out to be a position he would hold for 32 years.

Tiedman describes himself as a very nervous young man, but despite that, or maybe partly because of it, he had a longstanding passion for boxing, and intermittently throughout this early period the 6'2", 185 lb. artist not only drew, but jogged and sparred and handled himself very well in the ring, engaging in one of America's great midcentury sports romances.

Tiedman trained at the Old Angle Gym in Collinwood with Sammy Greggs, who had prepared heavyweight hopeful Ted Gullick (eventually defeated by George Foreman) for the ring just a couple of years earlier. Greggs thought Randall would have world class potential by going down a class in weight. He sparred at the Angle with Windmill White; he even boxed in Vietnam. Eventually Tiedman's ambitions faded, but not before he met and talked to legends like Floyd Patterson, Joe Frazier, and Muhammad Ali. He actually saw Ali three times, the last time during a promotional tour with Frazier at the Cleveland Arena.

There's no telling how important these early boxing experiences are to an understanding of the paintings Tiedman has produced in recent years; perhaps they're not important. Painters don't have to spend time in the ring (though as Tiedman reminded me, Picasso was fond of boxing) to master the kind of sparring with line and plane, color and substance that he does so well, or to convey the half-sick feeling that life's savor, its delight and detail, is kneaded with dull blows, and mixed with pain and sweat.

Tiedman's dark slopes combine a sense of limitless space with an intimate range of painterly techniques, engaging something like the mind's sense of touch even as they encourage the gaze to sweep to the far edge of forbidding prospects. Maybe that's the connection with the nighttime world of blood and cigar smoke and with the hard side of life on Cleveland's margins—Tiedman brings the reality of pain and disciplined brutality to his images, illuminated intermittently, pitilessly, as implacable forces rush and twist half-seen in deep shadow.

Time in the ring could be very much like time in a painting, then—a matter of accumulation and compression. Pain became a mark at the edge of the canvas, a triviality. Time stretches to the eyes around the ring, and snaps back to the gleam of muscle. Everything evaporates, effort and learning and hope, flattened on the hard surface of elemental need: to strike and endure is everything. The view in the ring, like the vista in any painting, has no real height or depth but is a seed of night, a point that marks the difference between before and after, fear and bravery, triumph and defeat.

Each of Tiedman's paintings is a world-class bout with paint and thought and age. And at 63, he's well ahead on points.

A Cleveland of the Mind: Or, Thirteen Ways of Looking at a City

Philip Metres

It was evening all afternoon.
—Wallace Stevens, "Thirteen Ways of Looking at a Blackbird"

1.

In Mark Halliday's poem, "Cleveland," the poet imagines "a single mother named Janey / waiting for a bus, trying to concentrate / on a science-fiction novel in the muddle of late afternoon." She is almost twenty-eight and has a six-year-old son named Harold. Once a beautiful woman who garnered triple-takes from passersby, she's now at the stage of life where she's just a "two-look" problem for men. In the poem, Halliday then admits he's made up this scene, from Philadelphia, which makes the scene even more uncanny—Janey in Cleveland, Janey as Cleveland. For the outsider, for Halliday, Cleveland is the place where you wake up to reality. As Halliday puts it, "she has become increasingly realistic in Cleveland / where you have to choose which reality to deal with when."

2.

The scuffed, the soiled, the scarred. The scalded arm of the short order cook now wrapped in a white cast, who watches his girlfriend shake her pitching arm in the sixth inning of work for the Carroll Blue Streaks, in University Heights. She's tiring. He'd give his arm for her if he could.

3.

The magnolia blooming on Magnolia Drive, and the hordes of wedding parties in black and burgundy tuxes, and ivory and saffron and powder-blue chiffon dresses, all assembling in rows for wedding album photos around Wade Park Lagoon. They play starring roles in a film about love and the need to voice it publicly. Matinees are free, all Saturdays from April to October.

4.

As longtime denizen Mike Danko related to me, when they were thinking up names for the new stadium megaplex, one was "The Inferiority Complex."

5.

Not the Shish Tawook sandwich I bought for a panhandler at the Falafel Café on Euclid Avenue, but the panhandler's sudden tears, as we sat at the shared table. This, after spending the morning examining the exploded base of Rodin's *Thinker* on the porch of the Cleveland Museum of Art—destroyed by an anonymous bomber in 1970, and never arrested.

6.

The stretch of Euclid from downtown to University Circle, where the ghosts of mansions fidget beneath the blight of warehouses and gas stations; the families wanted to take not just their memories past the outskirts of the city, but the houses themselves, wall by wall.

7.

Cleveland offers itself not as a single unified being, but as irreducibly multiple. Whosoever saith they know it, they know it not.

8.

One dark night, the twilight of yellow streetlamps echoed by the snow piled on sidewalks and slathering the street, and late for the Cavs game, I barreled through Ohio City, looking for an unfamiliar house, when I saw something glinting in the distance, in the middle of the street. Swinging his body down the center of the snowy street, a man on aluminum crutches.

9.

There are Clevelands I'll never know, nor want to know, and if I did, I would already be someone else.

10.

In January air, the beach at Mentor Headlands is primordial nature—the winds churning the surf, the gulls treading the air, not a soul in sight. But in the distance, when you move through the dunes toward the lighthouse, you cannot miss the huge chimney of the Perry nuclear power plant jutting on the coast further east.

11.

Because people prefer to shop in Legacy Village, a mall that has neither a legacy nor resembles a village, but has extra wide parking lots, I could no longer walk through Joseph-Beth bookstore on our way from parking lot to Shaker Square's Saturday farmer's market, to exchange cash for cheese from an Amish family.

12.

The grays, the innumerable and unnameable grays, the old milky gray, the mixing cement gray, the stone gray, the skinned knee gray—the skies of winter and all its gray guises, so permanent, when, suddenly, at five in the afternoon, the sun deigns to descend below the mask, and arcs a light so painfully beautiful, it snarls traffic for miles—the westbound commuters flying suicidal, into the cauldron of evening.

13.

As in Lawrence Ferlinghetti's *A Coney Island of the Mind*, or Sergey Gandlevsky's "America of the Mind," a place is as much inside us as it is outside us. Every daily path slowly burns its neural path into our brains, until each of us, a denizen of Cleveland, inescapably, not only lives in Cleveland, but comes to create a Cleveland, to become a Cleveland, a cleaved land, a place we cleave to, a place we are inextricably a part of and apart from, a Cleveland, a Cleveland of the mind.

Love Letter To Winter

Jonathan Wehner

Somewhere I read that the weather is a great topic for small talk. Stay away from religion, politics, and how much money you make. "How about this rain?" is the Miss-Manners-pre-approved topic of choice when you've got nothing else to talk about.

It has been unseasonably warm up here next to the lake for the past ten days. Warm enough to sleep with the windows open. And when I wake up, the warm air and the sound of waves crashing sometimes causes me to forget it is early December. They say we might have El Niño again. That potential prognosis reminds me of when you got sick in high school: "They say it might be mono," you said to me, and I said, "Who the fuck is 'they,' anyway?" Doctors? Nurses? Meteorologists? All sound equally ominous to me. So "they" say we might have El Niño again.

And I know the minute I tell you this I'll regret it, but this Indian Summer so late in the year makes me miss the snow a little bit. Not the dirty-crud-black-ice left over from a season's worth of Cleveland-style-torment—the other kind: the soft-centimeter-shoe-print, sweater-and-a-scarf, melt-on-your-nose-and-eyelashes kind.

"You miss the snow? Heresy!" shout the old-time neighbors, but this madness started when the block club put up those damn little lights. I guess you know, I'm a sucker for blinking-white-lights and garland strung up lamp posts. Still my growing-old-time brain can't quite make sense of these Christmas lights without the snow. "Winters on the lake," the old-timers say, "are brutal, and cold, and snowy, and lonely."

But tonight as I sit on the porch alone, sneaking a contraband cigarette, I'll stare out long into these lights. And when the wind kicks up suddenly and blows smoke in my eyes, I'll close them just for a second. And with the pinpoints of light burned into the back of my eyes like a constellation, I'll be swimming in memory. Like tonight, the air is warm, but the snow is an inch deep and falling. There I am in my father's old beige trench coat, two sizes too big. And with scarves and mittens and sticky-Chap-Sticked-lips we are racing away from the confines of suburban adolescence and out into the urban night. Up wafts the smell of greasy-diner-onion-rings, and Sampoerna-black-cloves, and exhaust from your Chevy that needs a tune-up. As we speed up 71 the Cure and Peter Gabriel blast out from our mix tape. Irving and Gardner are our new prophets, and we speak loudly as though *Reservoir Dogs* and *The Breakfast Club* are *Citizen Kane*. In the parking lot I mouth off to a cop who hassles us about our long hair, and inside you hope aloud that tomorrow is a snow day so you can stay in bed all day. And one movie, four cups of coffee and countless parking-lot-donuts later we proclaim youth is wasted on the young and deem this night completely forgettable. Then we each go home and lie awake in bed wondering where we'll be a decade from and wondering if we will still be together.

These smells and sounds of memory swirled around my head, thick like the morning after a night of too many drinks. Until I shook them off and asked myself "Is El Niño's Christmas gift to me a memory?" Funny that some warm water in an ocean I've only ever seen in pictures would make me recall such a day. Not my first day of school, or my first kiss . . . . Not my first concert or the day I met my wife. I guess it takes a meteorological event on the other side of the world to make me realize: after thousands of hangovers and broken hearts; after years of nine-to-five and five-to-two; after play dates and conference calls; after feet, and feet, and feet of snow, those days we thought were wasted would be the ones we wished to relive.

Now, sharing our memory is my gift to you. I know . . . it's kind of like the popsicle-stick-picture-frame you made for Mother's Day in kindergarten, and you are probably about as impressed as she was. But like I heard an old-timer say once in a movie, "I'm sentimental, and a lot of other people in this country are sentimental, too." And sometimes sentiment is all you've got.

The Seriousness of Vintage

Claire McMillan

"**T**hose ladies did not mess around," said my friend Linda, who at the time owned a now-defunct vintage clothing shop on Cleveland's east side. She was referring to Cleveland women from the '20s to the '60s who powered their shopping with the fallout from Cleveland's mining, shipping, and steel industries.

When I moved to Cleveland from San Francisco ten years ago, I received an education in vintage. Linda ran her store out of her ramshackle house, the only residence on a street lined with antique dealers and furniture consignment shops. She lived upstairs and sold clothes out of the crowded first floor.

I still wear treasures I bought from her because she was right—Cleveland women back in the day absolutely did not mess around. A black crepe Balmain blouse with trapunto stitched sleeves, a grey wool YSL cape with a tassel on the hood, a navy blue knit Courreges dress as heavy as armor and as confidence-inspiring, a gossamer blush-colored floor-length Hanae Mori that comes out about once a year when the invitation says black tie, a white canvas YSL trench, and a handful of smart cocktail dresses with Halle's and Higbee's tags sewn in them. Those fine old department stores, now long gone, were once the Bergdorf's and Barney's of Cleveland.

I bought multiple Bonnie Cashin coats—the good ones in Easter egg colors and made of mohair and leather with the turn locks. Lin da supplied me with Ferragamo bow flats—looking never-worn and in every shade. I run around town in them with everything from jeans to cotton dresses. These coats and shoes are symbolically Cleveland to me. Superb quality, practical, not flashy, pretty in a ladylike way with a sporty air so you can move and get things done.

When I got to know Linda, she told me she did the Manhattan vintage show each year. The first time she'd gone, she'd sold out completely before the doors opened to the public. She'd been thrilled. She was less thrilled when she saw her clothes in the neighboring dealers' stalls—they'd simply added zeros to her price tags. She'd since tagged everything with Manhattan prices before going back.

But it was too much trouble to retag everything once she was home, and so when you'd walk in she'd tell you everything was fifty percent off.

Such is the difference between New York and Cleveland pricing.

The first day I found her, I greedily bought everything in my size, amazed at my luck after a decade of San Francisco's vintage selection and prices. Two huge bags and enough on hangers that she followed me out to my car and helped me get it all situated.

Once she knew me and my sizes, I'd get phone calls.

"Just had some seriousness walk in the door," she'd say. I loved those phone calls, dropped everything when I got them.

Sadly Linda went out of business—despite thriftiness, my town is not a vintage mecca, though it should be. Linda never could get the hang of eBay.

It was years later when a friend called me with an unusual suggestion that I go meet a new saleswoman at one of the big national luxury department stores in town. I'd been noncommittal.

"Just go," my friend said. "Today."

Ann had worked for Christian Louboutin in Paris and then London and then New York. A native Clevelander, a series of life challenges brought her and her daughter back home, which is a very Cleveland story. The day I met her, she was in a black knit Adolfo with Chanel bow pumps. She loved vintage, was an avid thrifter. In addition to expertly guiding me through the designer racks, she graciously offered to keep an eye out for me when she went thrifting. I now had two kids and almost no time to shop. I gave her my measurements, and she told me she'd call.

A few weeks later, she had a little stash for me. I was to pick it up, take it home, try it all on, decide what I wanted, and bring back the rest at my leisure. We'd talk price later. What was in that first bag? A Giorgio St. Angelo dress, a red Kenzo silk dress, a YSL skirt, a little flannel Cacharel blouse, a liberty print sundress.

I tried it all on, kept everything that fit and sadly returned the things that didn't. Ann's prices were just as reasonable as Linda's. Anything I passed over, she put on eBay.

She invited me thrifting with her one afternoon. I'm not a particularly good thrifter, lacking both patience and vision, but I set aside an afternoon mostly because I liked hanging out with her. It was an education stepping into those vast hanger-like spaces with their stale, organic smell.

"Doesn't it freak you out?" she asked in a hushed whisper. "How many clothes exist in the world? Do we need to make any new ones? Unless, of course, they're art."

I was overwhelmed looking at the racks, but Ann was not. She was in and out in thirty minutes, going up and down the rows fast. Everything, I mean each and every thing she put a hand on, had a good label—old Halle Brothers, Bonwit Teller, Nan Duskin in Philadelphia—or a designer—Missoni, YSL, old Ralph Lauren.

"How the hell do you do that?" I asked.

She explained it was all in the quality of the fabric and that once you had an eye for fabric you could spot something worthy quickly.

Two Max Mara cashmere winter coats for less than twenty bucks total—that's what she pulled out for me that day.

She told me about the Japanese pickers she'd heard of. They'd start in New York with a shipping container waiting on the West Coast, rent an RV, and drive across country hitting up thrift stores. They, too, could whip through a store in thirty minutes like a SWAT team. They mostly wanted men's clothes—American-made denim, old flannel—and they loved the industrial Midwest. They loaded their finds in boxes and sent them to the container on the West Coast. When they made it to LA, they shipped the container to Japan and flew home.

I love wearing strangers' old clothes. I know it skeeves out some people, but I do wash or have them cleaned thoroughly. Whenever I find a heavy piece of old French-designed clothing here, it reminds me that my city used to be a metropolis. That housewives living in Shaker Heights knew good fabric when they felt it and bought quality over quantity. My city used to be able to support French fashion. I know the loss of high-service, local luxury department stores and the advent of mass-produced clothing is not unique to Cleveland, but reflects larger changes in our country such as a move toward casualness and quantity over quality.

When I put on my Courreges bought here, or my lady-like flats, or my chubby Cashin faux fur, I feel I am keeping a tiny bit of Cleveland's spirit alive—style and thrift, quality and authenticity. We make use of what we have here because we're thrifty like that, but also because back in the day people did not mess around. When they built houses, they built houses meant to last more than one hundred years. When they built and endowed the art museum, they endowed it to be free and open to the public always. When they bought clothes, they bought clothes meant to last decades, not seasons. Each time I put something old on, I'm keeping these clothes in Cleveland, not letting them be exported. I'm acknowledging the quality of the past and the wisdom of wearing it in the present. I am not messing around.

VIII. Back Home

Garie Waltzer

Why I Am Not a Boomerang

Joe Baur

ity boosters call people like me a boomerang, which I suppose I am—
but in name only. Cleveland was as foreign to me as any other
city in the United States when I was growing up in Mentor. If you
would've dropped me in front of my downtown apartment five years
ago, I would've been immediately and indefinitely lost.

Except for a few Indians games with my father and brother, I
never went from Mentor to Cleveland as a kid. I was scared of it. I
thought Cleveland was a behemoth, surely one of the largest cities in the
country, and dangerous to boot: a trip there was an invitation to get shot.

My older brother Dave heard this about Cleveland all the time:
"There were definitely a lot of my friends who thought you went to the
city to get shot," he recalls. "That was sort of the mentality of a lot of
the kids we grew up with. At best you drive downtown, get your ass to
Jacobs Field, get out and you're done."

Dave was less fearful than I, though, and he did explore the city.
He loved the Flats. "The Flats, I think, was one of the things that stood
out when I first started going down there."

The Flats was a bustling neighborhood he loved to visit for concerts and to spend time with his friends. "There was one time a bar band
was playing just inside the front door and the windows were open and
nobody was paying attention to them. And me and my friends stopped
to watch them play, so they ended up turning around their whole drum

kit and everything toward the street because we weren't old enough to go into the bar."

Dave also remembers taking trips to Case Western Reserve University with our father, who was an assistant varsity coach for the women's basketball team and who had grown up in Forest Hills. Ask my father about downtown back then and his face lights up as he recalls visiting the once-famous department stores that anchored downtown, May Company and Higbee's, and seeing the Sterling Linder Christmas Tree.

My father moved away from Forest Hills when his father, Grandpa Bud, made one of Cleveland's earlier suburban escapes and moved his family to Euclid. It was the '50s and racial tensions were rising on the east side. Crime was going up, amplified by incompetent government officials.

It's easy to look back and wish folks like my grandfather stayed in their neighborhood to *fight the good fight*.

But Bud lived through the Great Depression, surviving on the shores of Lake Erie in Hooverville tents. He wasn't about to watch his son endure the same life of poverty. My father made a similar decision, moving further east from Euclid to Mentor. Education was a priority for him, and he wasn't about to take a risk on a failing Cleveland school district.

As for me, after I graduated college, I moved to Chicago. It made more sense than returning to Mentor or to Cleveland, which was still foreign to me. But there was no sense of community in Chicago. My northside Chicago neighbors acted as if the city ended downtown, ignoring the west and south sides of town. Many of my neighbors were fellow transplants who moved to Chicago, as I did, because of some mirage of a better, more affluent life. But that only exists for a lucky few in Chicago.

Ironically, it was only once I had moved to Chicago that I became interested in Cleveland. While I visited my family in Mentor, I went to neighborhoods I never knew existed when I was growing up, like Tremont and Ohio City. In Chicago, my mornings were spent Googling about happenings in Cleveland. If there was a story on a new business opening in MidTown or a restaurant in Ohio City, I knew about it before I could look out my Lakeview neighborhood apartment to see the weather.

I wanted my money to go to Cleveland businesses, not Chicago ones. I wanted to spend it at the places I was reading about, like the

Happy Dog, Edison's Pub and Old Angle. I wanted my tax dollars—something we frequently forget impact cities when we leave them—to be spent on improving Cleveland schools and the Rapid.

Although I was still learning about the city, I liked Cleveland more than Chicago, more than LA, more than any other city I had lived in, traveled to, or would go on to travel to. The gritty feel of walking down Starkweather in Tremont with St. Theodosius Church towering over the former homes of steel mill workers mixed with the influx of new condos and businesses sprouting around the block resonated with me, and the echoes of our industrial history fueled my work ethic and motivation. I became excited by the community's enthusiasm for the Flats East Bank and Uptown projects. I loved the trite but true friendliness and genuine humanity I experienced in almost every interaction in the city. This, I realized, was home.

I moved back and embedded myself into the community my father had left almost 60 years ago. Now he and I enjoy new developments from Gordon Square to University Circle together.

Today, I know exactly where I am, who I am, and what I'm not. I'm not really a boomerang. But I am a Clevelander.

One that Denver Lost

Stephanie Gautam

> The child is an individual who loves whatever locality he is born
> in to the point that he could not be happy anywhere else.
> —Maria Montessori, *The Absorbent Mind*

As a child growing up in Cleveland Heights, I felt that my hometown was a paradise. The ravine off North Park Boulevard was just steps from our duplex on South Overlook, yet to me, it was a wilderness promising adventure and otherworldly discoveries. In the opposite direction, down Cedar Hill, was Little Italy, offering the comfort and delight of Mama Santa's cheese pizza—extra sauce and double cheese. When I was four years old, my mom and I started the annual pre-Christmas tradition of ordering Mama Santa's and taking it with us in our car to devour as we simultaneously took in the holiday light displays at GE's headquarters and Public Square. Rituals and places grounded my love for Cleveland as a child.

But the combination of glamour and contentment that I felt slowly slipped away as I grew up. By the time I was 16, it became cool to ridicule the place that you came from. I went to college near Cleveland at Denison in Granville, Ohio, and as I struggled to find my identity and claim my adulthood, I subsequently rejected the authenticity and toughness that comes with being a Clevelander. Not Rust Belt Chic, but simply: chic. I thus made it my mission to get out.

After I graduated college, my boyfriend Mike (also a Cleveland native) and I packed our car with our belongings and drove off towards the mountains and omnipresent sunshine of Denver. We didn't know a soul there, nor did we have jobs awaiting us. What we did have, though, was determination to experience life in a place completely different from Cleveland. We had only visited the city once, but on that August day, as we drove away from the grey, rainy Cleveland skies and toward our hopeful futures, we thought we would never turn back. Finally, I was leaving Cleveland.

Denver and its populace greeted us with big smiles and free spirits. Each day, we'd find people biking, hiking, and climbing, feverishly working to achieve the chiseled strength reflected by the Rocky Mountains. People parading the streets everywhere. "Ah," we thought to ourselves, "so many happy people out enjoying every drop of a vibrant, buzzing city." It really was a new and empowering experience to look toward the nearby mountains, to walk the streets of a beautifully maintained downtown with not a scrap of trash to be found. Troubadours lined the streets of the pedestrian-only 16th Street Mall, playing their own instruments or choosing one of the many elaborately painted pianos provided by the city. We felt energized by Denver. Most people we met were like us—transplants who had made the pilgrimage from the Midwest to Denver in anticipation of a bustling city life, endless sunshine, and proximity to the great outdoors.

But as we entered our first spring in Denver, the honeymoon began to fade. It was March. We had lived in Denver for seven months and I had not felt one drop of rain. I had not felt the glaze of humidity. I had not breathed in the distinct, earthy-thick smell that only comes with a Cleveland rain rolling in from Lake Erie. I was wanting and began to look about me, skeptical. Who were these people? Why were they here? Hardly anyone I'd met was from Denver. They had all chosen to flee their hometowns for this easy, college-like lifestyle, yet they all seemed lost, without purpose. I felt no attachment to where I was living. No deep camaraderie for the merry people I met. I longed for something real. I began intensely missing the people in the resilient city I had left behind. I ached for the Rust Belt Beauty I had abandoned. I craved the feelings of hope and turmoil that come with being a Cleveland sports fan. I missed the raw, soulful look of the old, dark buildings downtown. I heard the Lake lapping against the shore. I was homesick.

Staying true to the first phase that many of us from the Millennial Generation go through when grieving the end of a relationship, I began to stalk my lost love on the Internet. I spent hours glued to my computer monitor frequenting real estate websites and imagining myself living in one of the homes on the market. I would read *Freshwater Cleveland* and *Cleveland Magazine* everyday, fantasizing about being at the various weekend events in Tremont or Ohio City. I was eager to learn more about the Horseshoe Casino and the Flats East Bank development. I wanted to see what was becoming of Detroit Shoreway and the Gordon Square Arts District. I craved the taste of Great Lakes Christmas Ale and a #4 with extra hot sauce from Dave's Cosmic Subs on Coventry. I dreamt of being at Burning River Fest, Wade Oval Wednesdays, Tremont Farmer's Markets, and the Feast in Little Italy. Sometimes I found myself visiting the sites several times a day to ensure that I wouldn't miss an article on new developments. It was an addiction.

Then came the doozy. I began to realize that Cleveland was in the midst of revitalization. How wonderful: a resurgence! Hooray for the Rust Belt renaissance! Cheers to Cleveland! But then it hit me. Just as in a break-up. Or that crushing realization that your old flame is doing okay—no, thriving without you! I was jealous.

That's when I fell back in love with Cleveland. I pictured the lady's old brick buildings, abandoned warehouses, and empty steel mills, all poised against an unapologetic grey sky. It fed my soul. Part of my love is nostalgic. Part of it is wrapped up in my dreams for the future—to be a part of reclaiming my city. I decided it was somewhere I need to be. It's where my soul is. Then, as I was up one night reading a book, I came across this passage:

> In former times, in Italy, the people who were born in a village lived and died there and never moved away from it. Later people who got married sometimes moved elsewhere and gradually the original population were scattered from their native places. By and by a strange malady came about. People became pale, sad, weak, anemic looking. Many cures were tried but in vain. So at last when it could not be cured in any other way, the doctor said to the relatives: "I think you had better send this person to get a breath of his native air." And the person was sent to his home … and after a little while he came back fully cured. People said

that a breath of the native air was better than any amount of medicine. What this person really needed was the quiet given to his subconscious by the conditions of the place where he lived as a child.

—Maria Montessori, *The Absorbent Mind*

I decided to return.

Crossing the Ohio Border

Laura Maylene Walter

In December of my 21st year, I woke before dawn in Media, Pennsylvania, and grabbed the bag I'd packed the night before. I slipped out of the apartment quietly so as not to wake my brother and sister-in-law, made a quick stop for coffee, and then started the 425-mile drive to Lakewood, Ohio.

I was a junior in college just released on winter break and on my way to visit my boyfriend in his home city for the first time. I'd never made such a long drive by myself, and I was nervous. I wasn't sure how my car would hold up, or if I'd get lost once I entered the Cleveland area, or if I'd run out of gas somewhere in the middle of nowhere. I took Interstate 80, the lonely, mountainous route, and watched as Pennsylvania slipped behind me by the mile.

The drive made me think of my mother, who had always preferred I-80 to the Pennsylvania Turnpike and would take it even if it added hours to her trip. The last time I'd been on this highway had been with her, four years ago, when she drove me home from a summer arts program in Erie. I'd slept most of the way, leaving her to cross the expanse of Pennsylvania alone.

In the end, this drive to Cleveland was nothing to be nervous about. It was monotonous, long, one big yawn stretched out for hundreds of miles at a time. When I finally caught sight of the WELCOME TO OHIO sign stretched above the highway, I perked up. I pumped up the radio, danced in my seat. As I drove under the sign I waved and blew it a kiss—a little ritual I'd repeat, at least whenever I was alone, every time I crossed the border for years to come.

Why did it feel that I was coming home? I wondered this as I drove closer to a place I'd never been.

Peter had described in his directions where I could see my first glimpse of the Cleveland skyline: while crossing the bridge on Interstate 77. He'd made a joke about it, how the skyline was only three buildings, but to me this was a city. I could see it there in the distance through the passenger-side window, set solemnly against a background of winter gray. I was so distracted by it that a few minutes later I took a wrong exit and ended up in a gas station, asking for directions to get back on track.

The city flashed by in grays and blacks as I drove west toward Lakewood. I had only crossed one state border, but I felt so much farther from the restlessness and displacement I'd left behind. My mother had been dead not yet a year. Since then, I'd been moving around from place to place, rotating between college dorms, sublet apartments, and relatives' homes. For this one week in December, Cleveland would be as much my home as anywhere else.

The weather did not cooperate when Peter tried to give me a tour of Cleveland. We drove onto the Shoreway, where he'd hoped to show me a good view of downtown. What we got instead was slushy fog, a dense gray mixture of snow, cloud, rain, and cold. The buildings hovered hazy in the atmosphere, flickering in and out of sight. I leaned forward and stared patiently out the window. I could barely see anything: it was cold and miserable, the tour was ruined, and yet I loved it. Maybe I could belong in this city that struck me as humble but strong. Cleveland, I thought, was a place where people survived.

That week, we picked up a Christmas tree at the Y. We walked the family dog to Lakewood Park, and we had ice cream sundaes at Malley's. We drank $1 pints during happy hour at Rock Bottom at the Powerhouse in the Flats, and then we went downstairs to the arcade to play air hockey and Skee-Ball. Peter won me a stuffed giraffe. It was purple and had long, luxurious eyelashes. I knew I'd keep it for a long time, perched beside the blue bear some old high school classmates sent me after my mom died.

My mother had helped me pick out the car I drove to Cleveland—a green 1996 Subaru Impreza. At four years old and with 60,000 miles, it was the nicest and newest car I'd ever owned. I'd been nervous about spending all that money, but my mother told me it was a good decision. "This is a car that will at least make it through your time at college," she predicted.

Now 120,000 miles later, I still drive the same Subaru. It was the car I took with me to the D.C. area for my first post-college job, and it was the car I packed and drove away from D.C. when I finally moved to Cleveland for good. During that trip, I listened to Tracy Chapman's "Fast Car" on my tape deck over and over again. I didn't realize at the time that Chapman was from Cleveland. To me, during that drive, the song simply represented freedom.

Not many people in my life understood what Cleveland had to do with making my own way. They wondered why I'd leave a city like D.C. for Ohio, and they wondered what I saw in Cleveland. All I knew is that it felt right. Cleveland was gritty, honest, and tough. After feeling so adrift after my mom died, I suspected Cleveland would accept me as I was.

When I drove away from D.C. that last time, I didn't so much as glance in the rearview mirror. It was the only time I left a place without looking back, without worrying that I'd miss what I'd left behind.

During the first snow the winter after I moved to Lakewood, I left my apartment and walked to the park. It was snowing hard, coming in sideways from the wind, and I ran headlong into it. It wasn't like I'd never seen snow before—I was raised in Pennsylvania after all. And yet this was my first real Cleveland snow, the first time I saw it start to trickle down from my apartment windows, the first time I rushed to the fence bordering Lake Erie and watched it come down, white snow on white sky on white lake. It was all one thing, just like how those Cleveland buildings had faded into the fog years ago.

When I made it back to my apartment, the ends of my jeans and my socks and my shoes were soaked. My hair was heavy and tangled from the wind. I stretched my clothes out on the radiator to dry and then I sat on my thrift store couch. The radiators made me think of my grandmother's house. As a kid, I loved visiting my grandmother in Lansford, a failing Pennsylvania coal town. Sometimes my mom and I went alone, leaving my brothers and father behind. My grandmother cooked a vat of creamed spinach and the three of us sat together in her immaculate kitchen with the rotary phone and the bread basket and the clean white cabinets.

It didn't last, that first snow. It started heavy and then it stopped, and it didn't start again for weeks and weeks, not until we were deep into my first Cleveland winter.

My mother had been in the process of selling the house—my childhood home—when she abruptly lost her battle with cancer. In the weeks following her death, my brothers and I met at home on the weekends to clean, pack, and prepare the house for its new owners.

I'd never undergone a real move before, so I didn't know how to let go. I didn't understand the burden that came from possessions, how they create their own form of stress. I saved things that, years later, I'd unearth and hold up with wonder and frustration. Why in the world, I'd think, would I save this? I know now that I wanted to hold on to everything, as if a stack of boxes could translate to reclaiming what I'd really lost.

As far as I know, my mother never set foot in Cleveland. But I can imagine her squinting out at the lake on a summer day, her hand raised to her forehead to shield the sun. I picture each of us driving back and forth across Pennsylvania to visit each other, and how she'd no doubt travel the road that was longer but more beautiful.

Even now, 11 years after her death, crossing the state border makes me consider how my life has changed since my mother left it and Peter entered it. I try to imagine my mom at our wedding at the Lake Erie Nature & Science Center or offering advice when Peter and I bought our first home this year in Cleveland. I will think about these things and, if I'm driving alone, I might even raise my hand to the WELCOME TO OHIO sign as I pass it.

Sometimes, when I'm heading east and crossing into Pennsylvania, I wave to the Pennsylvania sign, too. But it means something different than when I greeted Ohio that first time. Waving to Ohio was my way of embracing what will come. Waving to Pennsylvania was honoring my past, my childhood. It was remembering where I came from and understanding that, no matter how many times I crossed that border, I couldn't go back.

Back then Cleveland was this dusty place on the horizon, the modest skyline I glimpsed out my window, and I could have passed it by but I didn't. Instead I moved there, motherless and cut free, and made that place my own.

A Cleveland Nationalist Comes of Age

Joslyn Grostic

I *am a long-time Cleveland Nationalist.* Like many nationalists, my early identity was greatly shaped by a cruel, misunderstanding world—a world that had cursed my homeland. It all started as a kid in the '80s. My brother and I were on a plane to Florida to visit family. The woman sitting next to me asked me where I was from.

"Cleveland," I replied.

Jokingly, she responded, "Oh, I'm sorry."

My throat closed up a bit and my stomach dropped. Did she just say what I think she said? For the first time I felt confused and ashamed about where I was from. But then self-righteous indignation kicked in. What did she know about Cleveland, anyway? A Cleveland Nationalist was born.

Of course growing up in Lakewood I felt no need to describe myself this way. Except for the trips to visit family in Florida, I rarely traveled out of town. Most of my contact was with Cleveland's near west side. Having nothing to compare myself to, I had little need to develop a Rust Belt identity. But even then it was slowly emerging as I began to make contact with the outside world.

As a teenage vegetarian, who regularly enjoyed eating at George's Kitchen on Triskett, I dined on grilled cheese sandwiches and hash browns. I had made friends with two young women who were visiting from Arizona. They were looking for lunch. I offered to take them to

George's and they asked me if they had salads there. "Oh sure," I replied. Their faces fell when they saw the waitress set down a bowl consisting of some iceberg lettuce and a pale, limp tomato. I ate mine with a cup of black coffee and a Marlboro red. I felt embarrassed that the salad wasn't up to their standards, but I also wondered why anyone would want a salad in the first place.

My Rust Belt identity really started to take shape once I went off to college. Antioch College was a diverse mix of students from all over the country. I proudly represented Cleveland. People often asked me to pronounce words like "Allison" and "apple" because they loved the sound of my nasally short A's—the little known Cleveland accent. I never quite knew if the sound of my voice was endearing or an object of ridicule. It probably fell somewhere in between.

As a young, environmental idealist, even I couldn't deny the raw beauty that lit up the night sky at the steel plant. When I would come home from school for a visit, the fluorescent emissions shooting from the LTV smokestacks were nothing short of a toxic art show. I was a gypsy, born to wander. But this was home.

Cleveland was downtrodden; it was beat up pretty bad. And, yet, there was so much magic in the misery. True beauty shines in the dark, overcast sky of a Cleveland winter's day. Even as a child, it was the most romantic sight in the world to me.

After college, I moved to the East Coast, where Rust Belt ignorance abounded. I swore to myself that I would never move back to Cleveland, but at the same time I fiercely defended my hometown to the core. It was during these formative years in my early twenties that I first publicly declared myself a Cleveland Nationalist. I would come back to visit good, old C-town and see t-shirts emblazoned with machine guns proclaiming "Defend Cleveland." Oh, how that resonated with me! This was a people who stood up for their homeland no matter what the cost. These were my people. People in NYC just didn't get it. Yes, they loved their city too, but there was no risk in loving New York. To love Cleveland took blood, sweat, and tears. Defending Cleveland took guts.

Although I never planned to live in Cleveland again, the irony is that in many ways I was recreating what I had left back home. I was never very comfortable hanging out with the "cool kids." Instead, I spent much of my time at a little dive bar in an industrial part of Brooklyn. At that time the patrons were mostly bridge workers and other blue-collar types, mixed in with some non-hipster artists. My people were the ones who liked to drink hard and remain anonymous. I learned about that bar from another Cleveland ex-pat. It felt like a slice of the near west side.

I remember the excitement I felt when it was announced that the Browns would be playing their first game since Modell had taken the team to Baltimore. I called the bartender and made sure that he would be showing the Browns/Steelers game at the bar that week. He promised he would. I felt chills as I sat in that Brooklyn bar watching Drew Carey introduce the Browns. That familiar sense of pride welled up inside me. That familiar sense of disappointment quickly followed as the Steelers proceeded to crush us. Of course, I just talked trash the rest of the night. Walk away with my tail between my legs? That just isn't the Cleveland way. We were total losers, but you'd never know it by the way I talked to everyone else in the bar.

The only time that I identified more as a New Yorker than a Clevelander was after September 11th. Watching the second plane explode into the World Trade Center, fearing for my life, seeing the missing posters all over town for weeks after: I felt inextricably bound to the people of New York after that ordeal. I came home for a week after 9/11, but I couldn't wait to get back to New York because it felt like I had left a big piece of me back there. As a Cleveland girl, this makes sense to me. It was the first time since I lived in New York that we were all going through a tough time together, and I tend to identify with tough times.

But my first daughter was born just one year later, and I boomeranged back to Cleveland. It would only be for three years to get my degree, and then I would head back east. My mom coaxed me here with the promise of childcare while I went to class. That was over ten years ago, and I have no plans of leaving anytime soon. I used to explain that I stayed here because Cleveland is a great place to raise kids. But lately, I'm seeing that this is a great place: period.

When I reflect on the Cleveland of my youth I still get that strange mixed feeling of claustrophobia and pride beyond measure. I guess I always will. We don't forget our past here. But we also seem ready to embrace a future that can both transcend and include our entire Rust Belt heritage.

A Vineyard In Hough

Mansfield Frazier

Editors' Note: Château Hough uncorked its first bottles of Frontenac and Traminette on June 1, 2014.

My *wife, Brenda, and I built our home* in the Hough community back in 2000. We married in 1999 while she was living in Dayton, and she made a new home part of the deal to move to Cleveland. We were fortunate in that we could have selected any community in the county to construct our new home, but decided on the inner-city neighborhood of Hough.

Why? My wife holds a master's degree in social work and I write about the problems of the underclass; neither of us wanted to be "arm's length liberals," folks who live in posh suburban enclaves while proclaiming to be dedicated to assisting those in need—but from a safe, comfortable distance. Additionally, we both knew we would hold little real political power or influence in exurbia; and besides, we hate commuting. So moving into Hough and attempting to recreate a vibrant middle class neighborhood was a natural fit for us. We were right, and now we have created a vineyard. Yes, a vineyard.

The revitalization of Hough had actually started back in 1987 when a black police captain, Billy Tell, built an upscale house on 87th and Chester, only to be ridiculed by some in the media for being foolish.

However, the idea caught on because three years later, in 1990, Renaissance Place, an entire couple of blocks of 20 upscale homes (built and occupied primarily by members of then-mayor Mike White's administration) were dedicated. The homes run between Hough and Lexington Avenues, from 73rd to 77th Streets.

Hough is perfectly situated midpoint between downtown and University Circle, about a mile from the front door of Cleveland Clinic. While urban planners at nearby universities scratched their heads in wonderment while predicting such housing would not work, the blacks behind the project knew it would.

By the time the houses were built, many blacks had by then come to the logical conclusion that housing integration was a chimera; except in a few isolated incidents, whenever blacks moved into a neighborhood whites gradually moved out. While integration is in itself worthwhile and noble, it still takes two races to integrate, and as long as one race is unwilling to do so, it simply won't happen. These middle-class blacks simply refused to debase themselves by chasing after something that was not achievable. The feeling is, if integration is to work, the door has to swing both ways. Whites who believe in it should be just as willing to move next door to blacks, who would love to have them as neighbors. Why should blacks do all the chasing?

The housing model worked so well that over the next couple of decades (until the crash) hundreds of new homes were built in Hough, and one key indicator of the strength of the market is that on the few occasions one of the homes has gone on the market it is sold in relatively short order. Nonetheless, the housing crash nationwide hit Hough just as hard as any other community. The question for us became one of, "What do we do with all this vacant land?"

Fast forward to 2010, when we established The Vineyards of Château Hough on the northwest corner of East 66th and Hough Avenue in 2010 with support from Reimagining Cleveland, a citywide effort to take vacant lots in neighborhoods and transform them into wide varieties of sustainable green projects. The cachet and positive attention the vineyard has brought to the community has been literally astounding. Neighbors getting to know each other by working together on an uplifting project makes for a much stronger social fabric.

Our non-profit organization, Neighborhood Solutions, Inc., brought together a variety of folks: community stakeholders; at-risk youth; volunteers from area universities; and most importantly residents of a nearby halfway house—to turn the three-quarter acre weed-filled lot into a vineyard capable of producing a total of 3,000 bottles of wine—half Traminette (white) and half Frontenac (red)—annually when the vines are fully matured in seven years. Our efforts have been generously funded by Neighborhood Connections, PNC Bank, the Charles and Helen Brown Memorial Foundation, and attorney Steven Schultz.

Bronx, N.Y. environmental activist Majora Carter is famous for saying: "You shouldn't have to move to live in a better neighborhood," and we believe her. Our overarching goal is to make the community we live in better by utilizing a variety of methods.

Indeed, the mission statement of our non-profit reads:

> To use innovative educational and entrepreneurial strategies to encourage, prepare and assist those returning—or who have returned—to neighborhoods after incarceration in creating greener, healthier and wealthier places to live, work, and raise families.

We feel we can combine our mission of wealth creation via job development with land repurposing and the national sustainability movement to utilize strategies that have proven to work in other locales, most notably Will Allen's Growing Power in Milwaukee.

One of the goals of urban farming is to grow as much food as possible within five miles of where it's to be consumed. By utilizing vacant inner-city lots, and unemployed formerly incarcerated individuals (along with at-risk youth), we feel wealth can be created for residents by locally growing crops and mastering aquaponics.

We selected vineyards as our initial project because they are perhaps the highest (and most complicated) form of farming, but also one of the most rewarding. Not only does the project draw attention, it raises everyone's vision in regards to what's possible on inner-city acreage.

We selected the name The Vineyards Château Hough to make a statement. If someone were to say Château Westlake or Château Hunting Valley no one would raise an eyebrow, but Château Hough rates a doubletake. It shouldn't, though, since the land we occupy in Hough is just as valuable to us as the land in other communities is to those who reside there.

Indeed, even if the wine turns out to be terrible, we've already won since neighborhood pride has increased, more of us know each other from working together in the vineyard, and the land value of the immediate area has increased, even if ever-so-slightly.

Our goal is to build on our success by controlling and developing more of the adjacent properties surrounding the vineyard. We've acquired an abandoned house immediately north of the vineyard and plan to turn it into a biocellar for crop propagation, while another nearby building is to eventually be used for fish farming. Both of these projects can be replicated in other neighborhoods.

As with any small non-profit, funding is always an issue and a struggle, but with the support and assistance of those who believe in what we are attempting to accomplish, we're confident we'll be able to successfully carry out our mission and make Hough an even better community in which to live, work and raise families.

Rust Belt regions cannot survive and thrive if urban cores are allowed to decay. Our decision to build our home in Hough stems from our desire to become urban pioneers and thus demonstrate in a palpable manner our belief that inner cities can and will make a comeback in America.

A Comforting Kind of Shame

Jacqueline Marino

I *became a mother on the West Side of Cleveland.* Two days after my daughter's birth in June 2004, I brought her home to a white colonial that was built in the late 1920s. It had a smoking porch overlooking our neighbors' vegetable garden and a red brick wall. Beyond the wall, Poor Clare Colettine Nuns prayed in seclusion, as they've been doing in Cleveland since 1877.

No one smoked on the smoking porch anymore. Not with a baby. Not with the nuns in eyeshot. Mostly, we paced up there. We didn't have air conditioning, and the fresh air, no matter how warm, seemed to calm her. I thought about a lot of things during that summer of sweat and sleeplessness, especially my own childhood in Boardman, Ohio, a suburb of Youngstown. While it's just an hour's drive east on the Rust Belt, I'd hoped it was a continent away in shame.

Modern sociologists, notably Anthony Giddens, say the role of place in shaping our identities is weaker now because we are "living in the world." Each of us is responsible for crafting our own identities. Perhaps where we're from shouldn't matter anymore, but it always did to me. Youngstown's location—between the one-time mob strongholds of Cleveland and Pittsburgh—and its profitable rackets made it a killing ground for organized criminals until the late 20th century.

Some kids get to brag about being related to famous actors, heroes or the founding fathers. I believed I was related to Roy "Happy"

Marino, a Youngstown gambler and racketeer who became one of the city's most notorious gangsters of the 1930s. He owned a nightclub on Coitsville Road, called the Town Club. He drove new cars, made questionable friendships and had both a wife and a girlfriend, one the newspapers identified as a "pretty ex-chorus girl." The son of a prominent Italian businessman, "Happy was a bad boy," one former acquaintance told me. "And he had no reason to be."

According to the Youngstown *Vindicator*, Happy earned his nickname "because of his reckless abandonment of worry." News of allegations against him, including fighting, bootlegging and theft, began appearing in the newspaper's pages in 1922. "Cracks Skull with Pool Cue," accused one news headline. "Whiskey Car Nabbed Again," blazed another. On June 10, 1933, three men dressed in farmers' overalls entered a bank near Canton. They pulled sawed-off shotguns from the basket they were carrying and robbed the bank of $11,000. Happy was convicted of the crime, but he served only 14 months before becoming a leading figure in a 1935 investigation of parole brokering.

My father said his aunts used to threaten him when he was a kid, "If you don't straighten up, you're going to end up like your cousin, Happy." My father didn't know Happy, only how he ended up: dead in a ditch in Columbiana County, his body riddled with bullets from a machine gun shot at close range.

As it turns out, I am not related to Happy. But when I was a kid, I wanted to be. I used to spend hours hunched over old family photographs, incriminating my male relatives. I imagined my great uncles and cousins holding cigars and royal flushes, cracking dice against backboards and blackjacks against skulls. I inspected their hands for burns, their fingernails for dried blood. I wondered which of these relatives had crushed the windpipes of double-crossers and affixed explosives to the undersides of Cadillacs.

If you're an Italian from Youngstown, people often think you have a relative like Happy. As recently as July 2000, *The New Republic* called the Youngstown area "a place, in the modern era, where the Mafia still held sway over every element of society."

Even though I read about it and heard about it, I didn't know this Youngstown when I was growing up in its suburbs, passing time at the mall, swimming at the club, enjoying weekends at my grandparents' house with the garden that took up most of the backyard. They grew almost all the vegetables they fed us. Big tomatoes bursting with juice, peppers the size of a meaty fist and thick stalks of glossy rhubarb flourished in dirt my grandfather tended—dirt he had moved himself in plastic bins from the house where my mother grew up on Youngstown's East Side. My grandfather was a gentle man, a math teacher who only threatened violence on the rabbits who feasted on his garden greens. His kids became professionals, too: a nurse, a doctor and a chemical engineer. We played bocce for fun and poker for pennies. We loved my grandmother's pizzelles and one another.

But as I grew older, I mostly just wanted to leave. The romance of being part of something very bad passed as soon as I was old enough to buy a bra. Soon after I graduated from college, I boarded a plane for San Francisco, a media darling of a city where I knew no one. After a year, I moved to Memphis to take a reporting job. It was thrilling but also lonely. I was beginning to miss being near my family and familiar places. When I thought about returning to Youngstown, however, a boulder seemed to roll into my throat. I had gotten out. Why would I want to go back? At the same time, I wondered why I pretended not to care about my hometown. After all, this was the place where my entire family grew up. My parents and grandparents, all their siblings. How could I hate the place and love the people?

On trips home to Youngstown, I began bringing my audio recorder to my grandparents' house. I learned about my maternal great-grandmother Julia, who once lied about being in labor so her husband wouldn't miss a day of work in the steel mill. She also delivered babies for other poor women, regardless of their race, ethnicity or ability to pay. Julia, a two-time widow with a fifth-grade education and six young children, spent much of her life scrubbing other people's walls and floors. But my grandmother, Julia's daughter Betty, said their Brier Hill neighbors helped them. The firemen next door left her sacks of flour on her front porch and paid her to wash their blankets, though their wives would have done it for free. Neighbors sometimes gave her kids money for bread, and my grandmother's teacher let her bring her little brother to school, so her mother could go to work. All of this kindness in the most corrupt city in America.

As I mapped the intersections of my family's history and the city's, I began to realize that the relationship between my relatives and their home—something I had downplayed in order to distance myself from Youngstown—was as complex as our relationship with one another. My mother and grandmother did not have any shame about being from Youngstown. They loved the area because they loved their families. They couldn't see the moral rot from their kitchen windows. They only saw one another. And goodness. And vegetable gardens.

Where we're from does matter. I think that's why I chose the pretty, old house near the nuns, a house that is more like my grandparents' house than my parents' one. Twenty years later, on the West Side of Cleveland, I saw the same things from my smoking porch. But I also saw beyond them—a great big web of connections. I want to keep the good I saw as a child in the lives of my children, the tomatoes, the trust and the simplicity. We may live in the world but not all the world feels right to us.

Cleveland feels right to me with its ethnic food, authentic charm and industrial landscape. It also has its own comforting shame in the burning river, embarrassing mayors and failed sports teams—even Mafia figures. But Danny Greene and John Scalish never defined Cleveland the way Joey Naples and Jim Traficant marked Youngstown.

Over time, the Mafia has lost much of its cultural relevance anyway. My daughter will probably romanticize powerful figures and try to see herself in them somehow, like other kids do, like I did. But those fictional figures are more likely to be vampires and superheroes than bootleggers and bank robbers. I'll take her to all their movies, but I'll be sure to make her visit the nuns in her first neighborhood, in Cleveland, too.

Hart Crane, Poet and Park

Anne Trubek

Life is awful in Cleveland.
> —Hart Crane, letter to Wilbur Underwood,
> June 15, 1922

H*art Crane, who is famous for having jumped off* the back of a boat at age 32 after having been lauded as one of America's greatest poets, is most often associated with New York. This makes sense: Crane lived and wrote there, after all, and his best-known work, *The Bridge*, is an epic about the Brooklyn Bridge. It is no surprise that the go-to biography of Crane, Paul Mariani's *The Broken Tower* (soon to be a motion picture starring James Franco), starts this way: "There was only one city for Hart Crane, and that was New York."

But this is wrong from the start. It's a Rust Belt story, that of Hart Crane. He even has a rust belt name—the name of a piece of heavy machinery—made even more so by the fact that sometimes he would sign his letters "Heart." Crane was not a New York but a Cleveland poet: a mess of a thing, a striving wreck of promise and all too human failings. Crane was raised in Cleveland and lived much of his short adult life in the city that made his father rich and his mother suicidal. He hated its over-obviousness, its out-to-make-a-buck spirit. "What especially irked him was Josephson's going gaga over Apollinaire's celebration of the new: 'the telegraph, the locomotive, the automat, the wireless, the street-cars and the electric lamp post,'" Mariani writes. "In Paris, such quotidian conveniences might be novelties, to be praised for their abstract design. But in Cleveland, such things were mere practicalities for getting things done or for getting from one point to another."

Crane hated Cleveland (or so he claimed), but he could not deny its traction. It had a "vulgar honesty" to it that Greenwich Village, already overrun by tourists and poseurs by the time he arrived there, did not. In New York and Washington, D.C., where he lived briefly when his father sent him to open new sales territory, he was often homesick. I have "a terrible vacuity about me and with me and a nostalgia for Cleveland," he wrote to a friend in 1920. It was not a beautiful place but he was happy there, he said. He returned home, and was relieved to be

> back into the usual smoke and tawdry thoroughfares . . . Does one really get so used to such things as, in time, to miss them, if absent? I am sure I should not miss factory whistles in Pisa or Morocco, but I frankly did miss them in Washington. Anyway, they were more enlivening (and the people they claim) than anything or anyone that I saw in Washington which seemed to me the most elegantly restricted and bigoted community I ever ventured into.

CRANE'S: A Store That Would Be Distinguished on Fifth Avenue
—sign on C.A. Crane's candy store in Akron, 1914

Hart's father, C.A. Crane, was a candy man. In 1901, cane sugar was the next new thing, so C.A. watered down maple sugar with it in order to make cheaper candy. He sold his sugar cannery to the Corn Products Refining Company. Then he decided cellophane was the *new* new thing; he was right, and got richer. He went to Canada and ate some really good chocolates, and by 1911 was selling "Queen Victoria Chocolates" all over Cleveland. Later it would be called "Mary Garden Chocolates," and he would have the painter Maxfield Parrish design the boxes.

C.A. also invented a hard candy that you could punch holes in. He called it "Crane's Peppermint Life Savers ... For that Stormy Breath," and put a picture of a sailor tossing a lifesaver to a girl on the wrapper. He sold the trademark for $2,900 in 1913 and the buyer went on to make millions with it. (If you know the end of Hart Crane's story, well, you'll appreciate the irony.

C.A. and Grace, Hart's mother, had a terrible marriage. They were always either fighting or having violent sex; their only son would later claim, according to Mariani, that this is why he never wanted a heterosexual relationship. After their first separation, Hart, née Harold, went to live with Grace's parents in an old Victorian house with two twin towers on Cleveland's East 115th Street. Hart would spend much of his life, as a child and an adult, in a room inside one of those towers. Today the house is gone, replaced by the Case School of Dental Medicine.

Harold was an indifferent student, attending Fairmount Elementary and East High irregularly. In February 1914, he attempted suicide twice: first he slashed his wrists and, when that failed, he swallowed 18 packets of his mother's sleeping powder. He also had his first homosexual encounter in high school, which, according to Mariani, "may have been a case of sexual abuse by an older man"—later he would talk about it to friends, sometimes changing the details to make himself the seducer.

Harold hated his father and, at the urging of his mother, renamed himself "Hart": his middle name, and his mother's. At seventeen he wanted out of Cleveland, and he left for New York. He would soon return. And he would repeat that pattern for another decade, coming back to Cleveland when he was broke and needed a job, or at the behest of his needy mother, or because he wanted to. He worked at a munitions plant on the waterfront, working seventeen-hour days six days a week tightening bolts. (C.A. always gave him lowly jobs to test his mettle, a test Crane always failed.) That job didn't last long—nor did his job as a camp counselor, or as a riveter for another war-related plant. The first world war ended right when it looked like he would be drafted. He wrote a poem about the armistice that was published in the Cleveland *Plain Dealer*, who then hired him as a cub reporter. He lasted seven weeks. He went back to New York, and then came back home again.

For a summer, Hart worked at a soda fountain in Akron, and the Akron newspaper did a story on him: "Millionaire Son Works In Drug Store." He became friends with another local writer, Sherwood Anderson, to whom Hart complained about his father making him work; Anderson told him to be more practical:

The arts [C.A.] ridicules have not been very sturdy and strong among us...Our books are not much, our poetry not much yet. The battle has scarcely begun. These men are right to ridicule our pretensions.

When the drug store gig ended, Hart's father transferred him to the Cleveland factory to unload chocolate and sugar barrels for 60 hours a week.

And then back to New York and back again to Cleveland, this time to work endless shifts at a shipping department. "Our age tries hard enough to kill us, but I begin to feel a pleasure in sheer stubbornness," he wrote to his friend Gorham Munson, trying to rally.

In Cleveland, he supervised bulk storage. He had affairs. He went out on "mad carouses" that began with "pigs' feet and sauerkraut" and ended in his tower, where he played classical music for his arty friends. At one point someone in town found out about his penchant for sailors and truck drivers. Crane paid $10 week, out of his $25 weekly wage, to buy the man's silence.

Crane loved boxing, which he described as "two sublime machines of human muscle-play in the vivid light of a 'ring'—stark darkness all around with yells form all sides and countless eyes gleaming." He wanted his poetry to be like boxing, to have a "patent-leather gloss," and "extreme freshness." He wanted it to hit hard.

By the time Crane was 23, the career-making poet-critic Allen Tate had dubbed him the greatest contemporary American poet. At 32, he jumped off the back of a boat. Some argue it was an accident, but most agree that he never grasped for the lifesaver.

> *A tugboat wheezing by*
> *Wreaths of steam*
> *Lunged past a sound of waters bending astride the sky.*
> —disconnected words from Crane's poems on
> a sculpture at the Hart Crane Memorial Park

After his death, Cleveland did not celebrate its native son: it judged him. A 1937 *Plain Dealer* article referred to Crane's "perverse personality" and "terrible psychopathic handicap that set him apart from normal men and women, and alienated the major portion of his intellectuals." In a 1962, the paper explained that Hart's homosexuality had led to his "alcoholic, shabby and hungry" existence. Even as late as 1981 they were dwelling on the poet's "sexual persuasion" in relation to his "alcoholic and sexual debauches."

Even without the bigotry in the way, Crane is a difficult man to memorialize. He was egotistical, quick to borrow money, usually drunk. His poetry is obscure, as he always made sure he was four steps remove from the real, and because he had to use feminine pronouns when he meant masculine ones.

Still, in 1995, more than sixty years after his death, the city of Cleveland finally dedicated a monument to Crane's memory: the Hart Crane Memorial Park—today "the city's most overlooked park," according to *Cleveland Magazine*. In this tiny alcove of a park are crammed six sculptures created by a local artist, Gene Kangas, and commissioned by the Ohio and Erie Canal. Two of the sculptures are a rather too obvious sky blue, thick curvy pipe-looking things. Others are forged form Cleveland's civic metal, steel. They curve, too—like the crooked river I guess—into half-ovals. Pocked with holes that make words, words from Hart Crane's poems. Not lines, mind you: scattered words chosen to greet the tugboats that sail down the river, in honor of the great failure of American poetry, the one who drowned.

I was there in June 2012 with about fifty other people, scattered under the bridges in a pocket park for Rivergate Fest, sponsored by the Cleveland Urban Design Collaborative. The party was to feature dragon boats, rocket cars and bands. I heard the bands but I never saw a dragon boat or a rocket car. No matter: they were selling beer, and the bridges above us looked like a Man Ray photograph left out on the rain. You know, rusted. Like the city, and like the jokes about it. And the bridge above us is, according to one overwrought academic study, the real inspiration for Crane's *The Bridge*. That's right but wrong: when tall boats drift down the Cuyahoga, that bridge draws up.

A bit too tipsy, plastic cup of Great Lakes beer in hand, I walked up to the couples and families and the young artsy types to find out what they knew about Hart Crane. A typical encounter: "Do you know who Hart Crane is?" "Who?" "Well, we're at the Hart Crane Memorial Park." "What the hell does that mean?" "The park is named after him." "No, I've never heard of him."

Only two out of twenty said yes. One said he knew Crane because he read about him on Purple Armadillo, a website devoted to gay and lesbian Clevelanders. The other said he knew the poet's name was because he hung out at the bar on the corner all the time, and one night he stumbled out to the park, perhaps to puke, and found the plaque in his honor. I forgot to ask him where that plaque is, and I should have, because I never found it myself.

No one much cared that they had never heard of Crane—no one responded to my questions with muttered excuses or "I really should have known that" or "Where can I find some of his work?" I like to think that if I was interviewing the same crowd in Brooklyn, I would have embarrassed some of them. The Clevelanders were not embarrassed. They did seem happy, though. Across the river, up a hill, sits a bar called Major Hooples. They project Indians games—and Browns games and Cavs games—onto the bridge pylon at night, lighting up the bridge with men dancing and hitting each other, for all to see. Crane, the boxing fan, would have loved it. Who needs the overwrought lines of The Bridge, the James Franco impersonation? Who needs to tilt their head to read on words like *"Far strum of foghorns Fog-insulated noises Midnight among distant chiming buoys adrift"*? The place knows itself. It is not trying too hard.

Even so, I would like to read this some day, while I am sitting safely inside a boat well stocked with lifesavers, floating down the Cuyahoga— someday soon, I hope—when Hart Crane and Cleveland no longer need to be reintroduced:

Follow your arches
To what corners of the sky they pull you
Where marble clouds support the sea wreck of dreams.

Hunting for Gain in a City of Loss

Richey Piiparinen

"A man is a god in ruins."
 –Ralph Waldo Emerson.

I *didn't so much grow up in Cleveland as I did into Cleveland,* like a vine wrapping around a brick. My thoughts and interests became tied to its physicality, to its familiarity, and with the familiar comes longing and nostalgia for the way things used to be: the buttermilk at the Market, my grandma's garden along the fence near the alley. But one memory in particular stands out.

As a kid in our yard behind our house on Colgate Avenue—I remember the Labor Day weekends. The pre-fall summer sat so clear with its temperateness: that sky so great and blue with an expanse holding birds like hands holding peas. The city air shows were that weekend, and we lived near the Lake. So each year we had a show in our own backyard, with the mechanical expressions of Blue Angels flying sharp and low, their sounds tailing behind them to give the auditory illusion of torn paper if it was bottled up and amped before being let out to scream. And while beautiful—the precision, this power—I was a little afraid of the noises. And it was then that I'd look to him, my dad, for reassurance: a sign it was okay. And there he'd be on the back porch looking up smiling at the force overhead. His face expressed because of feelings similar to the relief I got by finding him there.

Fast forward to the present and I still live in Cleveland, and that's the plus side of staying where you grew up: the closeness to memories can serve to give the past a presence. Yet there's a downside. The past can't exist intact. This is particularly true in the Rust Belt: the crumbling and abandonment and fires. The closings and leaving. All that physical deleting, then, serving as a constant reminder that so much of my past is gone. That my family as I grew up in it is gone. That my family as a father had just broken apart.

Sometimes the hurt is enough for me to want to leave Cleveland and start over. To say fuck it and make home merely a host. Because there's a certain wisdom in becoming unattached, and this is illustrated beautifully in the novel *You Can't Go Home Again*. In it, Thomas Wolfe writes:

> Perhaps this is our strange and haunting paradox here in America—that we are fixed and certain only when we are in movement . . . . And he never had the sense of home so much as when he felt that he was going there. It was only when he got there that his homelessness began.

Cleveland kills in that sense. We grow from a place real enough to know that though our feet are rooted on solid ground, our hands reach out into everything that rusts.

Across the smokestacks attached to the still, brick blocks that are no longer conjuring up a burn, across the sidewalks with people in heavy clothes, across the severity of a landscape that has had its face rubbed in it like the tired falling forward, I am only partially separate.

Don't get me wrong. I live as an individual. I am a father, a jogger, a writer, and a friend. I like cold domestics. Cook ribs and winter soup. I die hard with the Browns and play at being a hard ass probably more than those in my life can appreciate. To that end I live from where I was birthed. And in my living I affect in a small way the surroundings that bore me.

That last point has been clearly played out—how the Rust Belt city has shrunk. People get an urge or need to leave. They go. The city becomes still, partially derelict, and nature consumes. And then it gets called dead by those on the Coasts, with more people going to where the aliveness is said to be.

Yes, leaving has become common in America's industrial heart. It is easy to see why, as life is as real as a stone here. Fewer illusions. And it's nice to envision an escape—to Charleston with its walkability and beaches; to San Fran with its mist; to NYC with its buzz that can serve to keep the sound of aloneness away.

If fact I left once. I went to Chicago for a spell in my mid-twenties. I went there a year after returning to Cleveland from Ohio U. Remaining home after undergrad proved to be too much. Too many reminders and too much partying. Too many dead-end childhood friends. And I will always remember leaving Cleveland for an exciting new beginning. Driving across the Skyway Bridge and seeing the City of Broad Shoulders for the first time created a beat in my chest.

There, Chicago hummed. The amount of metal and movement and buildings not rotting due to inattention and emptiness, it sucked you in, like your body was whiplashed by constant waves of happening. And the outside energy served to drown your insides out, as there was so much shit to see and do. I studied psychology there. I hung out with hipsters in Wicker Park. Gang-bangers in Humboldt Park. I jogged Lake Michigan's liquid edge in the summer with a million others. But also its frozen edge in the dead of winter all by myself.

This of course brings to bear that paradox of huge-city living. Because the more you empty yourself into your outside the less of you is there to fill your inside up. Said writer Evelyn Waugh: "For in that city [New York] there is neurosis in the air which the inhabitants mistake for energy."

And I remember the night that this really hit me, or that leaving Cleveland for noise and action had simply made me lonelier, more withdrawn. Anyway, I was living on West Evergreen in Chicago's "Little Puerto Rico" neighborhood. It was summer. Shootings were happening as frequently as the sun came up. It was night, hot. Myself and a few neighborhood locals were drinking Mickey's on a roof. You could see Sears Tower in the distance. It was huge, untouchable: a man-made god pointing in the direction of where our heads cock when we aspire to be something beyond failingly human.

An extremely skinny and weak-looking Puerto Rican named Eugene was talking about the night he was shot. It was gang retaliation and it was the middle of the night and he was walking back to his mom's house, where he had lived, and still lived. He got shot from a car. He fell down. The person then walked over to him, stood over him: shot, shot, shot. While re-telling, Eugene would periodically turn toward the direction of the Tower as it lit Chicago's darkness. At one point he lifted his shirt. Up ran a scar from his waist to his neck. That story explained to me why Eugene—while present—usually wasn't. Rather, he was tucked in somewhere behind his zipper.

I was not unlike Eugene. Part of me was locked up for reasons not dissimilar. So I came back to Cleveland. Which meant revisiting those psychic geographies where my ability to be present was stuck in my past.

It has been nearly ten years since I came back. A near decade of living with the places that I grew up laughing and crying and screaming in. Years of living in the places that I still laugh and cry and scream in. And while I am far from perfect—far from whole—I at least know that what I am looking at is real. The Terminal Tower will always be my skyscraper. Sears will always be the impossibility of some illusion I can't reach.

So here I am, in Cleveland. I live not a mile away from where I grew up. One mile away from where a car accident took the life of my Cleveland-cop father just after we left an Indians game. A mile and half away from the house I used to live in before my recent divorce. Yet I remain here. Choosing to live with the vacancy and the abandonment and the loss, fighting to see the potential in it instead of just the need to escape.

I'm not alone. There are many who haven't left and fight to keep Cleveland going. Many who did leave and came back. Many who arrive. And many who remain away yet know that distance is just space, and that soul and birthright can neither be separated nor ignored by boundaries made of highways, hills, or self-imposed exiles. Cleveland: it kills in that sense as well. It tends to burrow inside of you like a room in your body you can't find even if you preferred to walk out.

I chose not to. I chose to return—and in doing so—walk back in so to speak. Too see everything, or as much as I can stand. If only to burn the smoke off my past so I can sense a place that no one or nothing can take away. That place? At the risk of sounding trite, it's called "home."

So here I am. In Cleveland. The Rust Belt.

Here in the presence of my daughter that I am raising to be a Cleveland girl, but a girl that will no doubt someday fight her own urge to leave. And regardless if she physically remains, here's hoping that she will always know home to be home, and not home as merely a host.

River on Fire

Stranger, the way of the world is crooked,
and anything can burn. Nothing impossible.
Who comes to send fire upon the earth may find
as much already kindled, may find his city
bistre and sulfurous. Pitched and grimed.
On those suffered banks we sat down and wept.
There the prophets, if there had been prophets,
would have baptized us in fire. Who says impossible
they fill his mouth with ash, they quench him
as if a man could be made steel. A crooked way
the world wends, and the rivers, and the prophets.
Go down and tell them what you have seen:
that the river burned and was not consumed.

—Dave Lucas

Acknowledgments

Dave Lucas gets all credit for making this expanded edition possible. Additional thanks go to Haley Stone, Jesse Miller, Bob Perkoski and Angela Bilancini. Without the contributors, who offered their stories and words, and the many readers of the original edition, there would be no first edition to expand. We are indebted to them.

Contributors

Huda Al-Marashi is an Iraqi American at work on a memoir about the impact of her dual identity on her marriage. Excerpts from this memoir have appeared in the anthologies *Love Inshallah: The Secret Love Lives of Muslim American Women*, *Becoming: What Makes a Woman*, and *In Her Place*. She is the recipient of a 2012 Creative Workforce Fellowship, a program of the Community Partnership for Arts and Culture, made possible by the generous support of Cuyahoga County citizens through Cuyahoga Arts and Culture. She lives in Rocky River, Ohio with her husband and three children.

Eric Anderson's book of poems, *The Parable of the Room Spinning*, is available from Kattywompus Press. He learned how to drive in the Flats in Cleveland; he would ride to work with his father, and as soon as they reached the top of the hill on Scranton, his father would hand him the keys and say, "Be back at 3 o'clock." Eric would ride around, looking at all the abandoned factories and bridges overgrown with vines, the small, leaning houses in Tremont, the great hulks of the steel mills girded by rail cars loaded with ore. He would think, "This is what the world looks like when it ends."

Roldo Bartimole has been reporting since 1959. He came to Cleveland in 1965 from Bridgeport, Conn. He worked at the *Plain Dealer* and

Wall Street Journal in the 1960s and started publishing his newsletter, *Point of View*, here in 1968 to 2000. In 1991, he was awarded the Second Annual Joe Callaway Award for Civic Courage. He was named to the Cleveland Journalism Hall of Fame in 2004.

Joe Baur grew up in Mentor, where he quickly learned t's are mostly silent. After spending a few months in Chicago post-college graduation, he and the city began to reject one another until he finally escaped to Cleveland to continue freelance writing, working on his political comedy venture Mildly Relevant News, and eating a variety of meats with a fried egg on top.

Chicago native **David C. Barnett** was 11 years old when his family moved to Fairview Park in 1963. At about that same time, he started using his father's reel-to-reel tape recorder to produce adventure dramas and disc jockey shows in the basement. David's subsequent radio and TV career at ideastream grew from these seeds, leading to many local and national awards. Now a Cleveland resident, he's profiled a number of Rust Belt icons, including d.a. levy, Daniel Thompson, and the Rev. Albert Wagner.

Pete Beatty is from Berea. He edits books for a living in Manhattan, but all his furniture and clothes are in Brooklyn (not the one in Cleveland). He writes and edits for theclassical.org. He is additionally @ nocoastoffense.

Lee Chilcote is a freelance writer who tells character-driven stories about the transformation of cities. His work has been published by Agence France Press, *Think*, *Land and People*, *hiVelocity* and *Fresh Water Cleveland*. Lee's relationship with Cleveland is complicated, and he doesn't really want to talk about it. If he had to, however, he'd probably mutter *"Cleveland rocks!"* followed by the soothing words *"post-industrial land of opportunity."*

Sean Decatur grew up in downtown Cleveland and Cleveland Heights, and now lives in Oberlin with his wife (also a native northeast Ohioan) and two children (both born in New England, but rapidly being converted to loyal northeast Ohioans). He works at Oberlin College as

Dean of the College of Arts and Sciences and Professor of Chemistry and Biochemistry.

Thomas Francis was a staff writer at *Cleveland Scene* from 2000 to 2004. He's a freelance writer now living in Chicago; his more recent work can be seen at ThomasFrancis.net.

Mansfield Frazier was born and raised in the old Central neighborhood of Cleveland. He took off to see the world as a bright-eyed 27-year-old and has lived all over the US, as well as in Canada and the Caribbean. After 30 years of what can only be characterized as a "checkered" career, he returned to Cleveland a published author. He currently publishes a magazine distributed in 20 states, and writes for *Newsweek/ The Daily Beast* and CoolCleveland.com.

Stephanie Gautam is a native Clevelander who moved to Denver for a lifestyle change following her graduation from Denison University in 2010. In her spare time, Stephanie can be found listening to old jazz records, perusing the internet in search of all things Cleveland, or eating chicken vindaloo. Stephanie lives with her boyfriend, Mike, and her pet rabbit, Lucy. After two years in Denver, they have all decided that there is no place that suits them better than Cleveland and so this August, they will make the trek back to their rust belt roots. They plan to move to Tremont and Stephanie will begin work on her M.Ed. at the Hershey Montessori Training Institute in University Circle.

David Giffels is an assistant professor of English at University of Akron, where he teaches creative nonfiction in the Northeast Ohio Master of Fine Arts Program. His most recent book is *All the Way Home: Building a Family in a Falling-Down House*. He has also cowritten books about Devo and Akron's rubber industry, and his writing has appeared in the *New York Times Magazine*, the *Wall Street Journal, Grantland, Redbook* and many other publications. His awards include the Cleveland Arts Prize and the Ohioana Book Award. A lifelong Akronite, he is currently at work on a book of essays about coming of age in the Rust Belt.

Denise Grollmus wwas moved by her parents from Los Angeles, California to Akron at the age of 12. Some might argue this was child abuse. Denise doesn't agree. Twenty years later, she's a writer and Fulbright scholar whose work has appeared in the *2006 Best American Crime Writing* anthology, *Good* magazine, *Salon*, *The Rumpus*, *Wax Poetics*, and various Village Voice Media papers. She was a staff writer for *Cleveland Scene*, and co-wrote *The Ohio Knitting Mills Knitting Book* (Artisan/Workman Publishing, 2010). Though she moved away in 2010, she swears that LeBron James is still dead to her, she'll never stop calling it "pop," and the answer is always: "We are DEVO."

Joslyn Grostic grew up in Lakewood (on the corner of Giel and Merl, across from the railroad tracks and Merl Bunts Park). After raising a ruckus at other points on the map, she made her way back to Cleveland. An aficionado of Noah's Ark, Joslyn lives with her husband, two daughters, and two beagles in Shaker Heights.

Nicole Hennessy is a nonfiction and poetry writer living in Cleveland, Ohio. Raised in Old Brooklyn, she spent her high school years in the suburbs. For her, leaving Northeast Ohio has never been more than a fleeting thought.

Kevin Hoffman wrote for the *Free Times* and was managing editor of *Scene*. He is now editor of *City Pages*, the alternative weekly of Minneapolis, where he lives with his wife, Erin, and dog, Winnie.

Dave Lucas is the author of *Weather* (Georgia, 2011), which received the 2012 Ohioana Book Award for Poetry. He has also been awarded a "Discovery"/*The Nation* Prize, a Henry Hoyns Fellowship from the University of Virginia, and Hopwood Awards in poetry and nonfiction from the University of Michigan, where is a PhD candidate in English language and literature. He lives in Cleveland, where he was born and raised.

Clare Malone lives in Washington, D.C and writes for *The American Prospect* magazine. Her work has also appeared in *Slate*, *Bloomberg*, and *GOOD*. She grew up in Shaker Heights.

Noreen Malone grew up in Shaker Heights (along with five siblings, including sister Clare). She now lives in Brooklyn, New York, where she writes for the *New Republic*. Her writing has also appeared in *New York*, *Slate*, and *Newsweek*.

Jacqueline Marino used to enjoy running in The Flats, but now you're more likely to find her running after her kids in a University Circle museum. An associate professor of journalism at Kent State University, Marino recently wrote a narrative nonfiction book about medical students at the Case Western Reserve University School of Medicine.

Claire McMillan is a native Californian and current Cleveland enthusiast. Her debut novel, *Gilded Age*, set in contemporary Cleveland, was published by Simon and Schuster in 2012. She lives with her family on her husband's family's farm east of the city.

Rebecca Meiser, a native of New Jersey, is no stranger to industrial landscapes. In Jersey, chemical "plants" were considered part of the state's greenery, but in Cleveland, Meiser has discovered organic zebra tomatoes, beauty in ruins, and a thriving writing community. Her work has been published in *Cleveland Magazine*, *Tablet*, *Cleveland Scene*, *New York* magazine, among others. You can view her writing at rebeccameiser.com.

Mandy Metcalf moved from the east coast to Cleveland in 2001. She lives in the Kamms Corners neighborhood with her husband Michael and her cats Mulder and Bianca. She works in the Ohio City neighborhood for Environmental Health Watch. She is an advocate for historic preservation, pedestrian-friendly streets, and Edgewater State Park.

Philip Metres moved to Cleveland in August 2001 to begin teaching literature and creative writing at John Carroll University, just weeks before 9/11. He's lived in University Circle (at the Quaker Meeting House on Magnolia Drive) and in University Heights, along with his wife Amy Breau and their two daughters. Author of numerous books (poetry, criticism, translation), his most recent book of poems, *abu ghraib arias* (Flying Guillotine Press, 2011), won the 2012 Arab American Book Award. Read more at philipmetres.com.

Milo Miller grew up in North Ridgeville and now lives in Rocky River. He co-wrote and co-produced the local independent film *Hero To* *morrow.* He is currently co-writing the *Apama* comic book which features Cleveland's first resident superhero since Howard the Duck (if Howard really was a 'superhero.') and is finishing another graphic novel that should be finished in early 2013.

Alissa Nutting is author of *Unclean Jobs for Women and Girls* (Starcherone 2010) and an Assistant Professor of Fiction Writing at John Carroll University. Her work has or will appear in publications such as *The Norton Anthology of Contemporary Literature*, the *New York Times*, *Tin House*, *Bomb*, and *Fence*. She lives in Lakewood, Ohio, with her husband and their two dog-children.

Erin O'Brien is a fifth-generation Ohioan and was born in Brecksville and grew up in Lakewood. She now lives on a half-acre field of dreams in Broadview Heights with her husband and daughter. Her eclectic nonfiction has appeared in *The New York Times*, *The Los Angeles Times*, and the Cleveland *Plain Dealer*. She also authored *The Irish Hungarian Guide to the Domestic Arts* (Red Giant Books, 2012) and runs an award-winning blog. Visit erinobrien.us for more information.

Kristin Ohlson was born in California's Sacramento Valley and moved to Cleveland after a year at Antioch College—the city's lush greenery and industrial artifacts were equally beguiling. She's written two books—*Stalking the Divine* (2003) and *Kabul Beauty School* (2007)—and is now writing *The Soil Will Save Us: How Scientists, Farmers and Ranchers Are Tending the Soil to Reverse Global Warming* (Rodale 2014). You can read more of her work at: kristinohlson.com.

Bob Perkoski is a freelance photographer, originally from Conneaut, Ohio, who has been in Cleveland for the past 14 years. "With its great architecture and culture," he says, "the city has a lot to offer visually. There's a photograph around every corner if you open your eyes and mind to it."

Richey Piiparinen iis a writer, urban researcher, and city strategist from Cleveland. He cares for the Rust Belt condition.

Laura Putre was raised in Parma and Seven Hills by an accordion-playing mom and a button-box-playing dad. Fortunately for her immediate neighbors in Lakewood, Laura does not play either instrument.

Jim Rokakis was born and raised on Cleveland's Near West Side. He ran for Cleveland City Council in 1977 at the age of 22. He expected to lose and begin law school that Fall. He won and spent 33 years in public office—nineteen years in Cleveland City Council and fourteen as the Cuyahoga County Treasurer. He spends his time now as the director of the Thriving Communities Institute, organizing land banks and raising money to knock down 100,000 houses in distressed urban Ohio.

Michael Ruhlman grew up in Cleveland, where he now lives. He has authored the popular culinary Chef series *The Making of a Chef, The Soul of a Chef,* and *The Reach of a Chef* and numerous other books, as well as *Walk On Water* and *House,* from which his contribution is excerpted. *Ruhlman's Twenty: 20 Techniques, 100 Recipes, A Cook's Manifesto* won the 2012 James Beard Foundation Award in the general cooking category. His most recent book is *Salumi: The Craft Of Italian Dry Curing.*

Jim Russell amassed his Rust Belt street cred in Erie, Pa. The cities of Buffalo, Pittsburgh, and (of course) Cleveland all exerted a powerful influence on his soul. Jim studies the relationship between migration and economic development from an expat perch in Northern Virginia.

Connie Schultz, a nationally syndicated columnist and essayist for *PARADE* magazine, has written about Cleveland for more than 30 years. In 2005, she won the Pulitzer Prize for Commentary for her columns in *The Plain Dealer.* In 2003, she won the Robert F. Kennedy Award and was a Pulitzer finalist for her series "The Burden of Innocence," which chronicled the ordeal of Michael Green, who was imprisoned for 13 years for a rape he didn't commit. She is the author of two books by Random House: *Life Happens—and Other Unavoidable Truths* and *". . . and His Lovely Wife."* She is currently writing her first novel, about a working-class class family, in which Cleveland plays a starring role.

Mark Tebeau, a professor at Cleveland State University, is an urban historian, digital humanist, and flaneur. He is writing a book about the Cleveland Cultural Gardens and American vernacular landscapes. He is the architect for the mobile application Cleveland Historical.

Randall Tiedman was born in Cleveland, Ohio on January 31, 1949 and resided in the Arts Collinwood neighborhood. Tiedman worked as a professional artist from 1982 onward. His work brought him a CPAC grant and is featured in several museum collections, including the Albright-Knox in Buffalo and the Butler Museum of Art. Tiedman died in 2012. This second edition of *Rust Belt Chic: The Cleveland Anthology* is dedicated to his memory.

Erick Trickey grew up near Detroit and has lived in Cleveland since 2000. He's written about Cleveland politics, history, people and culture for *Cleveland Magazine* for ten years and is a senior editor there. His reporting and writing has also appeared in *People*, *Agence France-Presse*, the *Utne Reader*, *The Plain Dealer Sunday Magazine*, and the *Louisiana Review*. He writes the *Cleveland Magazine* Politics blog at clevelandmagazinepolitics.blogspot.com.

Douglas Trattner made his way into food writing the usual way, via the practice of law, which he practiced in Columbus for seven years. In addition to his work in *Scene* (and before that the *Free Times*), Trattner is managing editor of *Fresh Water*, author of the guidebook *Moon Cleveland*, and co-author of Michael Symon's second cookbook *Carnivore*. He lives in Cleveland Heights with his wife, two dogs and, soon, chickens.

Anne Trubek is the author of *A Skeptic's Guide To Writers' Houses* and has written for *The Atlantic Monthly*, *Wired*, *The New York Times* and other publications. A professor at Oberlin College, she did time in Lorain County before moving to Shaker Heights in 2006.

Philip Turner is a longtime Cleveland-area bookseller who with his family owned and ran Undercover Books, with bookstores in Shaker Hts., downtown Cleveland, and Chagrin Falls. He moved to New York City in 1985 and began working as a book editor and publisher. His personal essays have been published in the *BN Review* and *PW Comics World*. He blogs daily at *The Great Gray Bridge* where he writes about music, books, publishing, media, culture, and current affairs.

Afi-Odelia E. Scruggs is a writer and digital journalist. She was raised in Nashville. She moved to Cleveland in 1993, when she became a reporter at the *Plain Dealer*. She's not at the paper, but she's still in town.

Ted Sikora has lived in Cleveland or Akron all of his life. In 2003 he began a multi-year journey of creating the feature film *Hero Tomorrow*. Ted was the director, co-writer, co-producer, co-cinematographer, and editor on the piece, which debuted at San Diego's Comic Con and played film festivals all over the world. He's currently creating a series of artist profile documentary films for the Cleveland Arts Prize, and he's the co-writer of the *Hero Tomorrow* spin-off comic book *Apama*.

Douglas Max Utter is a painter and essayist on the arts. He has lived on Cleveland's East Side most of his life, with a few years spent in New York, England, and (when he was very small) Australia.

Laura Maylene Walter is a Cleveland transplant originally from Lancaster, PA. She is the author of the short story collection *Living Arrangements* (BkMk Press, 2011), the recipient of Ohioana's 2011 Walter Rumsey Marvin grant, and has written for publications ranging from *Poets & Writers* to *Cat Fancy*. She and her husband recently bought their first home in the Cudell/Edgewater neighborhood, where Laura has both a writing room and a bright purple kitchen. She blogs about the writing life at lauramaylenewalter.com.

Garie Waltzer, transplanted from New York, has made Cleveland Heights her home since 1971. For three decades she made the cross-town drive to Cuyahoga Community College's western campus, where she helped develop the program in photography from its origins in the old Crile Army Hospital into the high tech labs of today's elegant Visual Communications complex. Winner of the 2012 Cleveland Arts Prize in Visual Arts, Waltzer's work has been supported by grants from the Ohio Arts Council and the National Endowment for the Arts and can be seen locally at Bonfoey Gallery. She is currently preparing a solo exhibition of her project *Living City* in Hong Kong in 2013.

Jonathan Wehner is from Dayton and relocated to Cleveland to attend Case Western Reserve University and has since neighborhood-bounced from Hessler Street to North Collinwood to Tremont before settling in Ohio City with his brilliant and beautiful (but Pittsburgh-born) wife and their misbehaved dog. By day he recruits new undergraduate students to CWRU and by night he consumes (and sometimes creates) Cleveland art, food, music, sports, and beer.

Chris Wise often descended upon the city of Cleveland for music and other mayhem as a teen. He currently teaches high school English and creative writing in the Akron area and lives with his wife and two children in Canton. This is his first published writing.

Annie Zaleski grew up in Rocky River, moved away and had adventures elsewhere, and now lives in Lakewood with her husband. A veteran journalist, her work has appeared in/on *Salon*, *Rolling Stone*, the *Los Angeles Times*, *Billboard*, *eMusic* and dozens more publications and websites. She can be found at www.anniez.com and www.cassingles.com.

About the Editors

Richey Piiparinen is a writer, urban researcher, and city strategist from Cleveland. He cares for the Rust Belt condition.

Anne Trubek is the author of *A Skeptic's Guide To Writers' Houses* and has written for *The Atlantic Monthly*, *Wired*, *The New York Times* and other publications. A professor at Oberlin College, she did time in Lorain County before moving to Shaker Heights in 2006.

About Belt Magazine

"Creator Anne Trubek has taken the loose idea of writing about the Rust Belt and expanded the catch-all category with a host of brilliant writers on any and all topics that affect us, be it United pulling its hub from Hopkins and what role Burke Lakefront Airport plays in the region, to moving essays on what it's like to grow up, live and work in Cleveland. It's the sort of writing you won't find anywhere else, both in scope and talent." – *Cleveland Scene*

"The decaying cities of the post-industrial Midwest can sometimes seem like a museum of things America used to make: cars, refrigerators, steel, televisions. But if a start-up in Cleveland gets its way, the region may help rebuild the market for another endangered product — long-form magazine journalism." —Jennifer Schuessler, *New York Times*

"'Rust Belt Chic' is a movement. That's according to a new online magazine out of Cleveland, *Belt Magazine*, that aims to address the highly specific and often superficial attention paid to a wide swath of deindustrialized America" —Bonnie Tsui, *The Atlantic Cities*

About
A Detroit Anthology

"*A Detroit Anthology* is one of the surprise hits of the year. While many books have been written on and about Detroit by writers who have visited, this anthology of prose, poetry, and essays is written by the metro area's residents themselves … it's the wide ethnic array of voices that truly shows the facets of Detroit life. – *Ebony Magazine*

"What Clark has done with these writers is shown that you can have a truly authentic Detroit experience, built from all walks of life. There's city dwellers, suburbanites, new comers to the city (and region), former residents, and people just passing through. In a city that often pits people against each other based on race, class, and geographic location (although this is often linked more closely with the other two factors), [*A Detroit Anthology*] this book brings everybody to the table to have a voice. – John Cruz, *The Urbanist Dispatch*

"What these writers share, despite their differences of age, race, gender, and temperament, is the understanding that one has to know Detroit's history before even beginning to imagine how the city might move forward. Rather than trying to explain Detroit, editor Anna Clark says she set out to capture "the candid conversations Detroiters have with other Detroiters." She has succeeded spectacularly – Bill Morris, *The Daily Beast*

To purchase *A Detroit Anthology*, visit
http://beltmag.com/belt_publishing/

About
The Cincinnati Anthology

"Intent on chronicling the place she's called home since 2011, McQuade went about masterminding *The Cincinnati Anthology*, a deft, well-considered collection of essays, illustrations and photographs that represents, as she writes in her intro to the book, 'the visions of those who have fallen madly in love with the city of Cincinnati, either for the first time or all over again.' " – Jason Gargano, *Cincinnati CityBeat*

To purchase *The Cincinnati Anthology*, visit
http://beltmag.com/belt_publishing/

Forthcoming

Dispatches from the Rust Belt: The Best of Belt Magazine Year One
(Fall 2014)

Cleveland Sports Anthology
(Spring 2015)

The Youngstown Anthology
(Fall 2015)

For more about Belt Publishing, see
http://beltmag.com/belt_publishing/